Memories
of
Lincoln

Part of the
Memories
series

*The Publishers would like to thank the following companies for
supporting the production of this book*

Alstom Gas Turbines Limited

Branston Hall Hotel

Bromhead Hospital

De Montfort University

Denby Transport Limited

Dixon and Hogg Limited

EEV Limited

Hill & Osborne

North Lincolnshire College

Simons Group Limited

First published in Great Britain by True North Books Limited
Units 3 - 5 Heathfield Industrial Park
Elland West Yorkshire
HX5 9AE
Tel. 01422 377977
© Copyright: True North Books Limited 1999

ISBN 1 900463 43 1

*Text, design and origination by True North Books Limited, Elland, West Yorkshire
Printed and bound by The Amadeus Press Limited, Huddersfield, West Yorkshire*

Memories are made of this

Memories. We all have them; some good, some bad, but our memories of the city we grew up in are usually tucked away in a very special place in our minds. The best are usually connected with our childhood and youth, when we longed to be grown up and paid no attention to adults who told us to enjoy our youth, as these were the best years of our lives. We look back now and realise that they were right.

So many memories, and so many changes: one-way traffic systems, pedestrianisation, self-service shopping. How strange it felt at first to pick up a basket (those were the days before shopping trolleys!) and help ourselves from the goods on display on the shelves - it was almost like stealing! The trend led eventually to out-of-town shopping in centres.

Through the bad times and the good, however, Lincoln not only survived but prospered. We have only to compare the city as it is today with its new shopping centres and up-to-the-minute facilities with the city as it was, say in the 1940s, to see what progress has been realised and what achievements have been made over the last 50 years. Lincoln has a history to be proud of - but more importantly, a great future to look forward to, into the new millennium and beyond.

Contents

Around the city centre

Every town and city has a distinctive civic landmark. You look at a photograph of it and you recognise the place. This surely must be Lincoln's Stonebow and High Street in the 1940s give a wonderful reminder of how grand this part of the city was then. The shops and businesses synonymous with this area, the crowds of shoppers, the inevitable policeman plus white gloves and what a contrast in those two vehicles. Shops like Foxs, Kendalls, Pratts and Samuels, which is still there today, were at the heart of Lincoln's trade. The Saracens Head, the Midland Bank and the Guildhall and Stonebow give us this 'feel' of Lincoln. This is the centre of the city both today and historically. The city council met here for over five hundred years. Above is the Guildhall and the Mayor's Parlour; in here are housed reminders of Lincoln's past. A real view of Lincoln taken at a time when there was a great feeling of optimism about. The war, while not forgotten, is in the past and there is a future to build. The people who have crowded into the city give us, as we look at this photograph, a feeling that they are of the same mind.

Above: A wonderful photograph of High Street in 1928 almost in its splendour. The tramlines are still functioning but the overhead wires and the trolley bus are more interesting. The bus has the dignity of a regal galleon carrying all before it rather than the more mundane function of carrying the citizens of the city. This dignity is maintained in the car, a model T Ford perhaps and also in the style of dress of men and women - the suits, the hats on both men and ladies, that cloche hat especially. Hepworths, the tailors on the corner of Cornhill since 1893, like all the other shops does have that air of easy grace which we my not see today. Lloyds, once the Capital and Counties Bank, has yet to lose its cupola. The Black Bull Hotel is here still open for trade at least until 1961, although it has lost its old frontage. British Home Stores will extend and remove that hotel from the map to allow for its extension up the street. Other famous names on this side of the street were Wyatt and Hayes, tailors until 1964, Dixons chemists and Wingad tobacconists. A picture of the old Lincoln in many ways.

Above right: No health and safety regulations, no hard hat area, no miles of orange tape here for any one working or spectating as a new telegraph pole is erected in Mint Street close to the Guildhall in 1900. The view is looking towards High Street and the spire of St Swithin's Church. Even without the pole this is an interesting picture of gas lamps,

shops, Hunters the accountants and in the corner the cabmen's hut. But this is a beginning, the coming of the telephone system, tied in with the building of a new Post Office. That is why the crowd is there. Other people working always attracts an interest. What is being done here was bound to be regarded with more than just interest. It would be viewed with a kind of awe, even fear of the unknown but there would be the excitement that these feelings often do bring. The age of instant communication is being introduced to the city. For the few at first, as computers were a few years ago for us. Many of us thought we would never have to use one nor learn how to. The same could well be the feelings behind the coming of the telegraph - 'Great idea but I'll never use it'.

Photographing this part of the city is a worthwhile exercise for this gentleman. He is capturing on film a view for which Lincoln is famous of the Stonebow from the south. It is a very quiet High Street on this occasion but there is a lot to photograph. Lincoln has always contained many buildings worth capturing on film even without moving away from this street. If our photographer is looking to record evidence of earlier times he does have a wealth of opportunity. It is often said that a resident of a town or city which does have a long historical past is sometimes unaware of that past or needs to be reminded of it. Then will come a response like 'Of course I remember now ' or 'I never knew that'. It often takes a visitor to jolt the memory or even to inform. Our photographer can find evidence of Roman ruins by the new City Hall where there are remains of the lower west gate through which goods would have been bought from Brayford Pool. Perhaps if he is interested in the Normans he will walk towards Steep Hill where there is still some of the architecture of that time. He can look at the medieval black and white half timbered houses behind him near High Bridge. The Stonebow arch was the southern gate of the medieval city of Lincoln. There is so much for the visitor to discover and so much for the people of Lincoln to appreciate.

A 1950s view of the High Street before pedestrianisation and the larger modern nationally known stores took over. Dunns and Kendalls and Mac Fisheries were known throughout the country but were sufficiently part of the city's shopping landscape as to be regarded as local while Fox's drapers was a true Lincoln shop. It is a feature of many towns that the Midland Bank does retain its traditional shape. There are exceptions and they stand out but by and large you know a Midland Bank when you see one and Lincoln's is no exception. It is hard to imagine that this is a main thoroughfare. Pedestrians and dog find life in this street at least more than tolerable. Yet there will be an explosion of cars and vehicles in the next 10 years or so. Every town and city has had to cope with this. How they did it and still retained the character and atmosphere of the place differed from town to town. The photographs of Lincoln in the 1950s and 60s do suggest there was something about the area that had to be preserved. To cope with the increase in traffic, the change in people's shopping habits and the rise of the larger stores often at the expense of smaller local ones, were problems for the planners. How well Lincoln managed that is for its citizens to say with all that experience behind them. To an outsider there is still in Lincoln a great deal of that character remaining from the past. Enough to say that the city appears to have coped well.

Above: The level crossing to the Midland Station was a feature of life in the High Street for many, many years. When the station closed in 1985 so the level crossing, much to the relief of many (but perhaps not the railway romantic of any age), was removed. The new Wigford Way ensured that the traffic could now move freely - though at the expense of a few of the city's buildings. The spire of St Mark's Church here was a feature of the city. Soon the church was to be demolished and replaced by something that many in Lincoln might consider more necessary, a shopping centre. At the bottom left can just be made out the Ritz Cinema, opened in 1935, closed in 1981, re-opened in 1984 and, like many cinemas throughout this land, not being used as originally created. The old Midland station closed on 11th May 1985 and the decision as to the future of the site was a matter of great discussion. What was put on the site of the railway was something less appropriate but, unfortunately, necessary these days, magistrates' courts.

A 1967 view of the Stonebow and High Street. The arch is still open to traffic. The road signs show how important the street is and the lack of traffic makes you wonder why. Looking at the position of that cyclist it must be a one way street by now! The summer wear of the ladies contrasts with the suits of the men but there is an air of easy nonchalance about the place. That will be eroded when, in a few years, cars and commercial vehicles force a re-think and pedestrianisation takes over in 1972. Richards here have taken over from Pratts and Waring and Gillow next door seems to be attracting some interest by its display. Pratts were wine merchants and in its day the shop possessed attractive bow fronted windows, not now noticeable in Richards. The wine business at this time had been here for over 110 years and the Pratt family played a prominent part in the civic life of the city. The original shop, together with the premises of TL Lidgett, was demolished in 1902 when Saltergate was widened. Lincoln had lost two fine buildings. Pratts stayed on as the corner shop. The Midland Bank at the corner of High Street and Mint Street was formerly the home of Hepworths clothiers and this building, extended between 1923 and 1926, was once the Lincoln and Lindsay Bank. If you think how many banks there were in the city all independent of each other and then consider the number there are today after merger and closures. Think of the District, Martins, Provincial, Westminster - they are somewhere to be found, only the names may have changed!

High Street towards Stonebow at its most tranquil. A solitary mini van, parked in the sunshine is one of the few vehicles about on this sunny day in the 1960s. Shopping appears to be a pleasant experience, almost a stroll. Cross the road as you please. Park your bike at the edge. Buy some fish at Mac Fisheries or even some Coleslaw for it was that shop which was one of the first to sell it here. Buy a new television from Gibbards, even one of those that show programmes in colour. There aren't that many about. Try to see what is on at the Regal Cinema formerly the Picture House and at one time one of eight cinemas in the town. Make a quick decision before Littlewoods takes over the site. A pot of tea and a cream cake at the High Bridge cafe or visit Woolworths. The store has retained its old sign and the upper frontage is not what we normally expect from Woolies, but it does here feel very much part of the street. It had been here since 1923 taking over the site of the Spread Eagle Hotel. Each section of Woolworths had at one time mahogany counters, like the old Boots store which also favoured that wood. In its heyday there were 60-70 staff employed in Woolworths and, in fact, since that date it had been extended on two occasions in 1931 and 1937 with a further one in 1962. Since then it has moved, the first time to an equally prominent position, the second to a more anonymous one in the Waterside Centre.

This part of High Street was known as 'Top of High Street'. Before the city's centre of commercial gravity moved south, this street contained many of the shops and businesses which were part and parcel of the life of Lincoln. Think of Boots' second floor cafe which was THE place to be seen. The coffee, the teas, the cakes, the functions, the evening dances, the last waltz... The old Boots was distinctive and almost classical. The goods were displayed in mahogany glass fronted fitments and remained like that until Boots left this site in 1973 and removed further down High Street.

> **HIGH STREET CONTAINED MANY OF THE BUSINESSES THAT WERE PART AND PARCEL OF LINCOLN LIFE**

Boots' shops today are generally more 'functional'. At least the original building has survived. Think of Mawer and Collingham with its 'well' which was supported by graceful pillars and was approached by a handsome staircase, or a lift if an elegant entry was out for the shopper. This shop offered free delivery to the city boundary and resisted the move towards ready-made fashions for ladies by maintaining its very successful dressmaking department. Look today at what was Mawer and Collingham. Then recall how dignified both stores would have looked at one time.

Above: When you look at this photograph taken in July 1959 this is how Lincoln was at that time - Pratts, Saracen's Head, Woolworths. But these buildings were there as the result of change. Pratts was at one time not at the corner of High Street and Clasketgate. The Saracen's Head had been extended at one time back into Saltergate. Woolworths was built on the site of The Spread Eagle Hotel. Changes will take place. It will not be long before the Saracen's Head will close, before Pratts become Richards and Woolworths moves to another site. The High Street will be pedestrianised. New shops and businesses will move into the area as they have always done. Eventually will come larger stores, multi-nationals and extensions to existing shops. Some have fitted into the city centre. Others by their appearance have not and look out of place, especially here in the High Street, one of the focal points of Lincoln. The street has, if we look at the photographs of it through the years, retained much of its distinctive style and vitality. It is a very pleasant place to walk in, shop even or watch what is going on and there is often a lot going on.

Below: The construction of the Pelham Bridge opened up the city's north-south route but what it did do, and probably still does, is to put a great deal of pressure on Broadgate. This photograph was taken before the road was widened. To accommodate this the Green Dragon was restored and moved back a yard or two. Today the pub has a wonderful picture of the monster on its pub sign but there is a school of thought that perhaps its name was at one time Green Dragoon which is more in keeping with local military history. Broadgate will retain the Drill Hall and the premises of Parker, White and Arnold but both serving different purposes. The Broadgate salerooms will disappear. Thorngate House, the home of Rustons Gas Turbines, will be built in 1966. Some things will not change like the sight of St Swithin's Church, although the traffic swirling past it these days certainly removes the feeling outside of peace and repose. Some things will improve like the view the traveller has of the Cathedral. You win with the view, you lose with the traffic - especially on Broadgate.

The view as you approach the city from the south is awesome. This 1963 view is as grand for other reasons. It is from the Cathedral not of it. In the foreground is the Usher Art Gallery opened in 1927 standing in its tree-lined grounds. To its right is housing which is now a car park.

Crown House stands between the Gallery and the new Co-operative buildings, with the library on Free School Lane and Greyfriars beside it. The graceful spire of St Swithins Church, together with the Library, certainly enhance this part of the city. The developments around Waterside have yet

to come of course. Sincil Bank, home of Lincoln City, can be made out in the background. The Cow Paddle forms another part of the background as do the Sheaf Iron Works. In the centre is Pelham Bridge, opened five years previously by the Queen and providing the city's southern sweep to the centre and north via Melville Street, Magpie Square and Broadgate past the Telephone Exchange and St Hugh's Church and up to Lindhum Hill. There have been some changes since this photograph was taken but the shape of modern Lincoln is very much in evidence here.

Broadgate in 1961 and a view of two buildings which for many years were a feature of the street. One other feature is how easy it was then to park your car. Parker, White and Arnold's bottling plant is to the left. It was known as a mineral water plant but the advertisement above the Triumph Herald suggests other interests. It was acquired by the Council in 1961 and now forms part of the excellent library. It is certainly a distinctive looking building well worth preserving, as is its neighbour, the Drill Hall. This was presented to the Rifle Volunteers in 1890 by Joseph Ruston, principal of the engineering works.

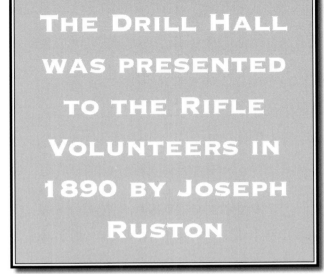

THE DRILL HALL WAS PRESENTED TO THE RIFLE VOLUNTEERS IN 1890 BY JOSEPH RUSTON

Ruston stipulated that 'in times of great distress in the city the Hall should be made available to the citizens'. In 1904-5 it was - during the typhoid epidemic which devastated the city and led to the deaths of 131 people. Then the hall was turned into an emergency hospital. In recent years the Hall has ceased to be used for the purposes for which it was built. Bingo, roller skating, exhibitions and meetings have taken over. The famous flagpole has disappeared and, unfortunately, today the hall has not retained the grandeur seen in this photograph. The increase in traffic is one of the reasons for that.

At leisure

An asset to the city which has been lost was Wickham Baths seen here in 1963. Its shortcomings were obvious. It was an open-air pool. The changing rooms at one time were wooden huts which may not have had a roof. The pool's concrete floor sloped in from the edges, at the foot of which was a stout metal rail running along three sides with one end being a kind of wooden platform. It was described as Lincoln's uphill bath. The unheated water was frequently covered with green algae. The pool's popular day was Tuesday for that was clean water day, the bath presumably been emptied on a Monday. Despite that it was still an asset. It was the place where the people of Lincoln learned to swim.

It had opened in the 1920s but over the years after the war it had fallen into disuse. The growing demand for swimming led to it being re-opened in the 1960s, as we can see here. In 1967, despite financial cutbacks, the council roofed the pool with tough plastic and, as there was only one other indoor pool at the time, it was very popular. But plastic roofs were considered dangerous and the pool closed for two years. Even then its final demise came as early as 1975. The pool was closed for safety reasons and three years later it was demolished, the site being handed over to the then Westgate Middle School. A bitter end to an amenity so much remembered for so many reasons.

Right: Every town and city has a hotel at its centre which is, as once described, 'the pulse of the town'. Easy to understand what that writer meant. If we agree with him, The Saracen's Head performed that function for Lincoln. A old coaching inn, situated in the city's busiest street, close to offices and businesses, private and public, close to the rail stations - so never a more likely candidate. It had grown in size over the years, with its buildings having been extended back into Saltergate. No expense had been spared in the 1920s and 30s to make it a first class hotel. From then on it was in its pomp. Its main entrance was described at one time as a 'riot of greenery' as plants festooned the walls and ceiling. They were everywhere. The Saracen's Head Tap was on Waterside North and was a very popular meeting place, especially during the second world war when locally based RAF servicemen would frequent the hotel. The closure of the hotel in 1959 was a great disappointment, especially to those who regarded it as a permanent fixture in Lincoln or to those who had some treasured memories of the place. The old frontage is still recognisable. Shops are there now inevitably, but the memory is allowed to linger on.

Below: A 1962 view of the Theatre Royal looking up the side of the King's Arms yard. Like all aspects of cultural life in our towns and cities the theatre was soon to undergo many a crisis, including the threat of closure. Saved by the Lincoln City Council in 1976 and then placed in private hands it has survived. The comeback show was the musical 'Singing in the Rain', described as the biggest and most expensive the theatre has ever seen. Since then it has had a succession of 'star' names to fill its seats. Think of Omar Sharif in 1985, though only to view, not to take part; or Raymond Burr (who played Ironside and Perry Mason), paying a similar visit. Remember who has performed in this theatre - Patricia Phoenix, David McCallum, Michael Redgrave and Jess Conrad. Fraser Hines and Colin Baker were to become regulars. Recall the plays, such as 'The Lion in Winter', 'The Darling Buds Of May' and 'Who Killed Agatha Christie?' and the extravagant' Rocky Horror Show'. And the necessary balance has been maintained. The locals have been given their chance- the Scouts, the local Amateur Societies, the repertory groups. The Theatre Royal has been described as the city's 'little gem' - an apt description.

The BBC's role in the war could not be underestimated, especially in the area of boosting workers' morale, thus hopefully spurring them on to even greater productivity. 'Music While You Work' was a very popular feature and 'Worker's Playtime' was broadcast three times a week from factory canteens during the lunchtime break. Here artists from Entertainments National Service Association, better known as ENSA, put on a show for the employees of Newsum and Sons in Carholme Road. They were entertained by Esther Coleman and Tony Brandon with compere Stephen Williams. By 1943, when this show was broadcast, 250 factories had been visited, 330 programmes transmitted and 27,000 workers entertained. Vera Lynn, the nation's favourite, appeared on the 200th show from a factory in the west of Scotland.

There were many other radio shows, including the very popular 'Brains Trust' and Tommy Handley's 'ITMA'. There was even a war time soap opera called 'The Robinsons' and the quaintly titled 'Ack Ack - Beer Beer', which featured talent among the men of Anti-Aircraft, Balloon, Barrage and Searchlights units, a forerunner of 'Works Wonders' perhaps. All designed to keep the workers happy and content. 'Workers Playtime' which of course continued after the war, had that aim in mind - to help to increase production. So, after taking the mickey out of the work's foreman, everyone sang at the end of the show 'Side by Side', about not having 'a barrel of money, maybe we are ragged and funny, but we're travelling along, singing a song, side by side'. In the words of the comedian 'Ay Ay, that's yer lot'.

A memorable day for all the wrong reasons. 18th March 1964 and the running for the last time of the Lincolnshire Handicap at Carholme. The first running of the race was on August 10th 1849 over two miles, different from the straight mile event it was to become later. At the height of its popularity the crowds to the course were vast and the Lincolnshire was one of the season's most colourful and popular races. But in the 1960s racing had begun to take stock of itself. The Horse Race Betting Levy Board announced that Lincoln's course was one of twelve not considered suitable for investment. The course and its appointments had been allowed to deteriorate to such an extent that it was described as having 'poor amenities, making it unpopular with all racing interests and the public', a sad indictment of the council's Race Committee. In 1966 the big race was transferred to Doncaster and Carholme was left with a few point-to-point meetings but minus two of its three fine grandstands. For the record Lord Roseby presented the cup on this last running of the Lincoln to Mrs G Lambton, the owner of the winning horse, Mighty Ghurka (33-1). It was ridden by P Robinson and trained by Teddy Lambton. There were 45 runners. The bookmakers at least were happy on this sad day for Lincoln.

Schooldays

Below: Thirty-eight children from the Oxford House School at 25 West Parade in the garden of the school. The boys are in their blazers trimmed with braid and the girls in their summer dresses mostly plain but some are patterned. They do not look as though they are allowed to smile. We can assume they are 'under orders' or, more than likely, they are just nervous of the camera. After all it is 1925. The principal at this time was Miss M G Brunner. She remained there until 1952 when the school was purchased by Mr C W Perkins and he kept it open until 1965. When you look at this group of children aged about nine or less, you realise the photograph was taken over seventy years ago. These children have now gone through school, work, marriage, presumably had children and grandchildren of their own and been successful or otherwise. Sometimes you look at photographs of your own class or school and pick out the other pupils the ones you know about. You know about their lives after school days. What about the ones about whom you have to say 'What ever happened to him? Or her?' It is a bit like that with this photograph. Wonder whatever happened to that group of thirty-eight children? They would all have a story to tell.

Above: The 1951 edition of the school look a lot happier than their predecessors of 1925, same garden, same blazers, same dresses almost. The only hope is that everything else has moved on a bit. These children are now in 1999 and in their 50s and like the 1925 group will have made something of their lives. They will still remember those schooldays. At one time there were four private schools in the city as well as Oxford House. Choice of schools was important for parents in those days as it is today. Generally, in the 1950s you either were educated privately or you went to your local school and then sat the 11-plus. Things are a bit more complicated now. Schools in the public sector can almost advertise for pupils - the official information map of Lincoln has 17 schools giving information about themselves. Competition for pupils is probably the reason. Education has become 'political' and the schools are no longer 'secret gardens'. There are school league tables now no matter what sector they are in. Oxford House, had it been open today, would have had to join the 'race'. Wonder how it would have fared?

> **AT ONE TIME THERE WERE FOUR PRIVATE SCHOOLS IN LINCOLN**

The Oxford House children in dress for a production of 'A Midsummer Night's Dream'. Perhaps they are only doing the part with the fairies. Then they can be Oberon and Titania and their train of followers. There is Puck, known as Robin Goodfellow, he with the ass's head. He is a shrewd and knavish sprite who would play comical pranks in the neighbouring villages. He would get into the dairies and skim the milk. There is Cowslip, Peaseblossom, Cobweb and Mustard Seed. These children will have had great fun being fairies and

sprites; whether they could unravel the whole play which centres round a law in Athens giving its citizens the power of compelling their daughters to marry whomsoever they pleased is another matter. How Hermia did not wish to marry the chosen Demetrius and favoured Lysander and was to die for the sake of her love. Still acting parts and playing and dressing up in costume seem to have come naturally to these children. They can look back and say 'I was Puck or Titania or Cobweb and I enjoyed it'.

Above: 'Do you remember that time when...?' That means there is usually something worthwhile to recall. With these boys it is success on a football field. It is a great feeling for any child to have achieved success as a result of his or her own efforts rather than be spoon-fed, then that is called 'achievement'. These boys of Skellingthorpe Road Middle School have every reason to look pleased with themselves. They have completed the 1954-5 football season as league winners and the holders of the Festival of Britain Cup, inaugurated presumably in 1951. The school itself opened in 1930 as the Skellingthorpe Road Junior Council School with Miss A E Newman as Headteacher. She was succeeded in 1941 by Miss N Gibson, who obviously would have been very pleased with these boys' exploits on the football field. The school celebrated its 50th anniversary in 1980. Praise for the parents in those years who helped to dig foundations for the swimming pool in 1962, stocked the library and provided camera and video equipment. Even the last remaining playing frame was welded by parents from scrap metal. As in all good schools the support of the parents is a natural and welcome part of school life and the success of these boys is a part reflection of that. This was a good year for the school team. Schools often have year group which is more outstanding than others. Then things happen. It appears obvious that this year group could produce 18 boys who helped the school have such a good season and bring to the teachers, parents and themselves a sense of satisfaction as a result of hard work. School league tables would have had a different connotation then for these boys.

Right: The members of the Bookworm Club had occasional visitors to the library who would read to them extracts from his or her books and prove that authors were real life people and not someone locked in a room somewhere churning out books. Douglas Duff was one visitor and he had the advantage of coming from a real-life place not far away - Mablethorpe. He generally put his naval title, Commander, in front of his name. He was actually born in Argentina. He had served with the Cunard Line and was in 1917 the only survivor of the sinking of his ship, 'Thracia'. Another claim to fame was he held a title of Officer of the Order of the Crown of Rumania. However he was obviously better known as a writer of adventure stories like 'The Miracle Man' shown here, 'Sword for Hire', 'Bailing with a Teaspoon' and 'Poor Knight's Saddle'. The increase in children's awareness of literature in the 1950s and 60s began to produce an increasing number of fine authors specialising in children's literature. The influence of clubs like the Bookworm Club was immense and the net began to spread. Schools and parents began to realise the value of good fiction which did more than assist them to become Uncle Mac's 'good citizens'; it helped children to appreciate language and characterisation and plot. And it gave opportunity for reading for pleasure. After all that is why adults read fiction.

Lincoln's new Children's Library was opened in the 1950s and was described by the Chairman of the City's Library Committee as a 'means of combating horror comics and pernicious literature that has found its way across the Atlantic'. The library was officially opened by Derek McCulloch, known to generations of children as Uncle Mac of 'Children's Hour', on weekday radio between 5pm and the 6 o'clock news. He was the voice of Larry the Lamb and much more besides. He had a place in the hearts of the children who grew up with him and would race home from school to be sure not to miss the programme. To the programme's many listeners he was like a kindly uncle.

McCulloch left the BBC in 1950 but returned in 1954 to be the host, often a rather tetchy one, for the next ten years of 'Children's Favourites', live every Saturday morning. Think of 'Nelly the Elephant' and 'The Laughing Policeman' and 'Tubby the Tuba' and 'Sparky's Magic Piano'. He was chairman of 'Nature Parliament' and subject of 'This Is Your Life' as far back as March, 1964, a month before 'Children's Hour was dropped. At the Library's opening he said that the new library 'belonged' to the children and how pleased he was to be part of this great day and went on to commend the Library Committee for its foresight and imagination.

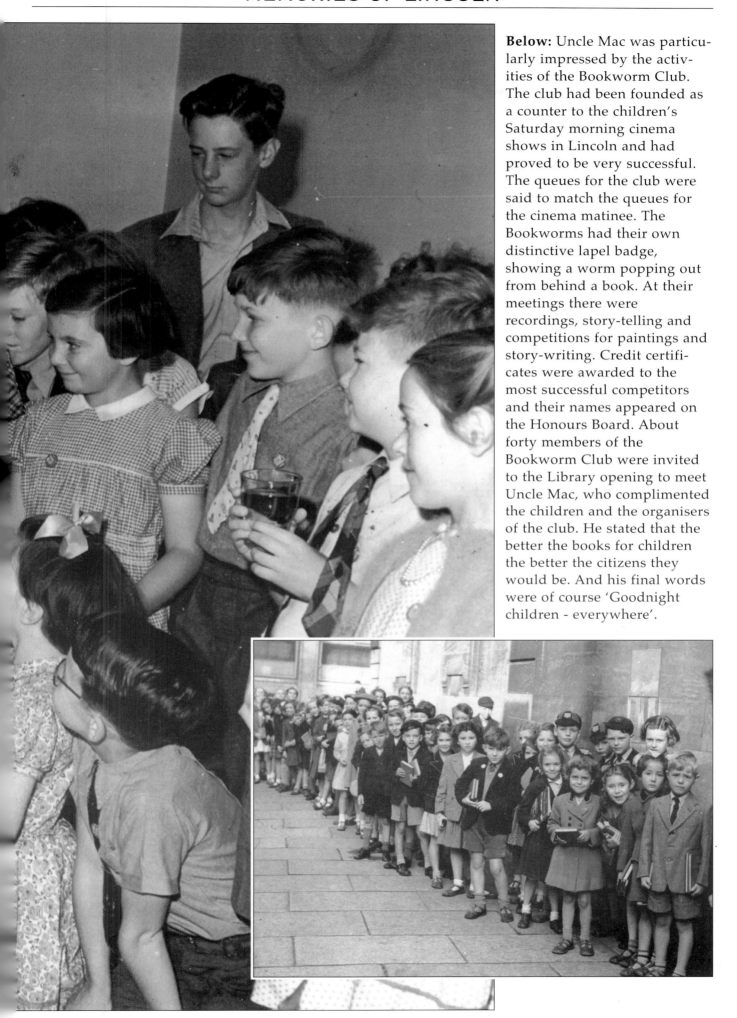

Below: Uncle Mac was particularly impressed by the activities of the Bookworm Club. The club had been founded as a counter to the children's Saturday morning cinema shows in Lincoln and had proved to be very successful. The queues for the club were said to match the queues for the cinema matinee. The Bookworms had their own distinctive lapel badge, showing a worm popping out from behind a book. At their meetings there were recordings, story-telling and competitions for paintings and story-writing. Credit certificates were awarded to the most successful competitors and their names appeared on the Honours Board. About forty members of the Bookworm Club were invited to the Library opening to meet Uncle Mac, who complimented the children and the organisers of the club. He stated that the better the books for children the better the citizens they would be. And his final words were of course 'Goodnight children - everywhere'.

Below: *The Coronation of our present Queen Elizabeth II took place in June 1953 and for the second time since the war the country could celebrate, The Festival of Britain two years earlier had taken the nation's mind off the war, rationing and austerity; the crowning of the young Queen gave the nation a chance to let its collective hair down. What a celebration! Not since VE Day had there been an excuse for a party and these children of Skellingthorpe Road Infants school were not going to be denied. Their teachers and helping mums are on hand to help in every possible way. It is hard to imagine that it was only three years earlier that soap rationing was ended and the 5/-(25p) limit on meals in restaurants and hotels was abolished. Everyone made a real effort to give the children a good time, though food rationing continued until July of the next year. But parents and teachers coped as usual. Children were not to be denied. A young Queen with young children of her own; a country waiting to blossom. These children have a lot to celebrate with their tea and games and their Coronation mug.*

Right: *You can imagine a child relating to his or her mother what had happened in school today and saying things like 'We played shops. I was the shopkeeper and sold some Toblerone, Bird's Eye custard and packets of sweets. They had to be weighed. We only used pretend money but it looked real. We sold toys as well. And we had to wrap them up'. A parent might these days understand the significance of the activity. But this photograph was taken in 1953 and schools were not as open in those days and parents might not have been so well informed unless St Faith's was a particularly enlightened school all those years ago and kept its parents up to date with the new methods of teaching number. This was the time of new thinking in schools about how to teach and what to teach. As long ago as 1944 the Ministry of Education, as it then was, advocated children having plenty of experience of number not only in counting but also in different kinds of measurement.*

It stressed the importance of using practical work as an aid to teaching. So the parents of children in St Faiths could have been reassured that the school was doing the right things then. And the children were enjoying their learning at the same time. They continue to do so if the recent Ofsted report is anything to go by.

The children of Birchwood Infants School sit down for lunch in their brand new sparkling school. The school, opened in 1965, was described as being years ahead of its time in architectural design, interior layout and teaching methods. This was a time nationally of new school building as the boom in the economy allowed many local authorities to replace old buildings, which had served their purpose, with more appropriate structures. The 1960s was a time of change in what children were taught and how they were taught. A great debate ensued and still does, of course. In Birchwood School there were no corridors. Each classroom had an outdoor terrace. There were movable fitments to divide the rooms into smaller areas.

Controversially - there was no set timetable, and even more controversially the headteacher, Miss M A Sewell, did not classify children according to age. Instead brothers, sisters and family friends were put in the same class even though their ages differed. Each class was made up of smaller groups, thus, according to Miss Sewell, enabling a family atmosphere to be created. What a debate there would have been at the time. To some these ideas would be just what was needed, to others heresy. The children would not join in the debate, of course. And looking at the photograph they seem happy about their school. It is often the case. Those on the receiving end of change in education often have to get on with it.

Events & occasions

A different view of High Street than the ones usually given. Apart from the horse fair we can see the Lindum Restaurant and across the road, still with tramlines, the Queens Hotel and just below the Corn Market what used to Barclays Bank. It is the Horse Fair that attracts the interest. The fair was usually held here on the Monday and Tuesday of the last week in April. The High Street from the Stonebow to the railway crossing was full of horses, often spilling over into St Mary's Street. On the Wednesday the fair moved to Broadgate and continued until the end of the week. Whitakers Almanac described it as 'the greatest fair in England'. Horses were lined on both sides of the road and if a purchase was being debated they would show off their paces by trotting down the middle of the street. It was estimated that as many as 800 or 900 horses could be sold on the first day alone, some staying in this country, others going abroad. A favourite trick, often practised by a seller, was to put ginger round the rear of the horse to be sold to make it appear more lively and alert. By 1929 the fair was transferred to West Common and during the war was held in the cattle market. It returned to West Common after the war but the demand for horses was not what it was. In 1952 not one horse was sold and the fair fell victim of the times.

Left: The people of the city gather on High Street as the civic procession winds its way through Lincoln for the Mayor to proclaim that upon the death of Queen Victoria, her son, Albert Edward, was to become King Edward 7th. The death of the much loved Queen was not unexpected for she had lain ill at Osborn House on the Isle of Wight for some time. Regular widely read bulletins regarding her condition had been issued. There had been some improvement in the previous week but as a local newspaper's headline stated there was 'continued anxiety'. In these days of instant communication it is often difficult to comprehend that then the newspaper was the only source of information for the public. News of her death on the Monday reached Lincoln the next evening by telegram. Immediately the city went into mourning. All public buildings flew the national flag at half-mast and there was general feeling of great sorrow. By the time for the proclamation on Saturday 26th January 1901 the mood had lightened a little. It was to be read out at six sites in the city and had been delayed until the afternoon to allow 'the workmen to attend'. The procession was made up of civic dignitaries, Sheaf Works band, Ambulance men, Church Lads' Brigade and boys and masters from the Grammar School. At each point the Mayor read the proclamation and called for three cheers for the new king. At one there was a shout from the crowd 'And one for Queen Alexandra'. That received a great cheer. Then the party returned to the Guildhall to drink the health of the King. Lincoln had paid due respect to the late Queen and to her successor.

Above: Ancient and modern meet as the 'new' bus meets the 'old' tram. Large crowds have gathered to say farewell to the tram service which had been operating in Lincoln since 1898 having replaced the horse-drawn tram. Following the inauguration of the city's bus service in 1920 the future of the tramway service was always in doubt. Overhead wires replaced tramlines in 1919 but by 1929 the end had come. The bus service had acquired a modern fleet and was attracting more and more passengers. So on 4th March of that year the last Lincoln tram began its journey. It was gaily decorated with flags and streamers and made its journey to the Bracebridge depot from St Benedict's Square at 3.30 pm with the Mayor, Councillors and Chief Officials on board. Three other trams followed, filled with members of the public. Mr Charles Hill was in charge of the first car with the Mayor and Town Clerk on the footplate. En route a collection was taken in aid of the Lincoln County Hospital. The end of the tramway era. Lincoln moves forward as it tries to provide a service which meets the needs of the time.

The highlight of the Civic Week held in Lincoln from 22nd to 29th September 1935 was the grand procession through the streets of the city. The procession was designed to show off all aspects of civic life and here we see one part - the agricultural one. This was a momentous year for the country as it was the Silver Jubilee of King George 5th and for Lincoln the centenary of local government in the city. The days of the old corporation had come to an end in 1835 and it had been replaced by an elected council. This civic week was described by the Mayor, Councillor J K Fox, as a sort of municipal stocktaking when the city would 'turn over the goods, plush them up and put them in the front window so that all may see what we have to offer'. The council's aim was to remind the citizens and maybe itself that it was 'the duly elected directors of your trading undertaking'. The week's activities were all designed to show that and began with a service in the Cathedral on the first Sunday. The official opening ceremony took place the next day, conducted by Alderman C T Parker. Public buildings, including the Cathedral, were floodlit and there were to be competitions for the best decorated streets and best decorated shops. The week had begun.

THE DAYS OF THE OLD CORPORATION CAME TO AN END IN 1935

Below: Every day in the Drill Hall there was an exhibition of all aspects of civic life. Each municipal department exhibited something. The range of services the council was responsible for in those days was somewhat different from that provided today. The Electricity and Gas services were municipal undertakings; the electricity department exhibited ancient and modern kitchen equipment and the gas showed appliances from varying periods. The Sewage disposal department entitled its display 'Evolution of methods of waste disposal'. Other displays came from the Police and Fire Brigade, Maternity and Child Welfare and Education as well as from other sections. All corporation depots were open for inspection at various times in the week. Wednesday was called 'Civic Day' and the 1,000th house built by the corporation was opened by Arthur Greenwood MP.

Children's sports were held on the same day and bands played in the evening at the Arboretum and in Boultham Park. Thursday was 'Shopping and Bargain day'! On Friday judging took place in the competition for best decorated shops, houses and streets. This busy day was completed by a municipal ball in the County Assembly Rooms with admission being 2/6d.

Bottom: There were other competitions during the week, including estimating the number of units of Electricity and Gas would be used in that week, the number of bus passengers carried and the number of books borrowed. There was a balloon competition and each day there was an exhibition of work in the City school and the Girls' High School. The final Saturday was the highlight. This procession of decorated vehicles was to show the various aspects of city life, industrial, agricultural, social and cultural. Every organisation and business was encouraged to take part. There were prizes for the best decorated horse drawn and motor vehicles, for cycles, for prams and carriages, for the most original fancy dress for adults and children. There was a separate competition for the best tableau, horse drawn and motor. The week did not finish there. On the following Monday or Tuesday, depending on the weather, there was to be a mass rally of the city's schoolchildren at the Arboretum, a fitting end to a momentous week, with a looking forward to the city's future with the next generation of its citizens.

Above: The people of Hood Street stand outside St Andrew's Church Parish Hall to celebrate the Coronation of the new King, George VI. Like all coronations it was a time for the nation to be happy and for events like this to be held in every community in the land. So the flags were put out and parents and neighbours tried to ensure that the children could share in the country's joy. Not many of these children, however, would know then the story of how this man came to be King. This was the time when the country put behind it the memories of the three hundred and twenty-five day reign of George's brother, Edward VIII. In the previous year their father, George V, had died. Edward succeeded him only to abdicate rather than end his association with an American divorcee, Mrs Simpson. It is hard to imagine today that such a situation causing the turmoil and grief that it did then. But there was national distress and Edward's 'final and irrevocable decision' for the sake of a woman he said he loved had all the hallmarks of a second rate Hollywood movie except it was true and it was so important to the country and to the Empire. So a shy, retiring man was thrust on to the throne. The whole country breathed a sigh of relief and the celebrations were long and heartfelt.

Above right: The adult residents of Hood Street would say 'We are only doing it for the kids' as they treat the children to a tea party to celebrate the end of the second world war in Europe. So out came the flags and the bunting. The tables were set out, chairs and stools found from a variety of sources. Tablecloths were pressed. Mams and grans, together with an occasional grandad, set out to entertain these smiling children with maybe at this time of shortage potted meat sandwiches. buns, jelly and pop. A Victory cake would more than likely have been baked. That would have meant sharing coupons. Of course it would be decorated in red, white and blue. Afterwards there would be games to be played, races to be run and songs to be sung. No more worries about air raids and the threat of bombs. All is needed now is for families to be re-united, with dads, brothers and uncles to come home from the war safely. The future belonged to the children and these adults were determined that they would not have to endure what they had gone through for the past six years.

The children of St Faith's Infants School are suitably attired to celebrate like every other school the Coronation of Elizabeth 2nd. And there is plenty for them to eat and drink. Those five lads in front look as though they were determined to enjoy it as are all the other children as they pose for the special photograph. Memories of that time vary from how many parties you attended, and what happened to your Coronation mug, to the holiday you had for the Great Day itself,

Wednesday June 2nd - and if you could get near to a television set to watch the day's events, filmed in black and white. They might remember it rained. Perhaps there was a street party or one in the church hall. Whatever occurred it was a memorable time for these and all children. There were enough reminders of that day to ensure they did not forget. So many years later, nearly 50, even these children could today recall something about the Coronation.

Lincoln celebrated the Coronation of Queen Elizabeth 2nd in June 1953 with 'two weeks of gaiety'. There were parties and carnivals, processions, dancing and sports. Public buildings were floodlit, streets decorated and shops dressed overall. At Brayford Water there was a grand display. 'Merrie England' was performed at the Arboretum, open air dancing in Boultham Park and on the eve of the great day Coronation Balls were held in the Co-operative Hall and the Assembly Rooms. June 2nd was described as 'TV's finest hour'. The test card was shown from 9.30am until 10.15 am and from then there was unbroken coverage of the procession, the ceremony itself and the events afterwards. This was indeed a great occasion for television and brought some great sights to those who had previously had little or no experience of this new phenomenon. Who can forget the crowds braving the unseasonal weather? The splendour of the ceremony in Westminster Abbey? The quiet, solemn moment of crowning? The joy afterwards as visiting dignitaries from all over the world were recognised and were not just names any more? The smile on the face of Queen Salotte of Tonga? No public events were held in Lincoln until the evening, allowing young and old to be glued to the set. Then there was a carnival on West Common and a procession round the streets of the city. On South Common there was a Punch and Judy Show, a women's football match, the ceremonial Beating of Retreat and to round it off a bonfire and fireworks display. The following days saw a Folk Dancing Festival at the Castle and Championship sports at Sincil Bank and the official opening of the Arboretum extension. That and many more street parties. The country had come alive. Gordon Richards, the nation's favourite jockey, riding Pinza, won the Derby for the first time in his long career. Edmund Hilary and Sherpa Tensing had climbed Everest and later that Summer at the Oval Dennis Compton hit a four to backward square leg off Lindsay Hasset's bowling and England won the Ashes. What a day! What a year!

Left: The visit of Her Majesty the Queen and Prince Phillip on the 22nd June 1958 was to open the new Pelham Bridge as well as to carry out other engagements. The Royal Train had spent the night outside Sleaford. Here we see the Royal Party being greeted by civic and county leaders in the form of the Mayor, Councillor L H Priestley, and the Lord Lieutenant, the Earl of Ancaster, as they leave Central Station. The weather was not kind to say the least! In fact it was so wet that outside the station in the forecourt one concerned onlooker was heard to loudly implore the Queen to 'Lift Your brolly, Miss'. It was not the sort of day that had been planned. It is supposed to be fine in June. Changes had to be made to the programme. No matter the weather the welcome from the people of Lincoln was tumultuous as the crowds stood beneath the rain drenched flags and bunting and the dripping streamers and baskets of flowers, whether it be on Lindum Way, at Pelham Bridge or outside the Cathedral. At the Cathedral the Queen and the Duke were shown the Cathedral's copy of the Magna Carta, the most priceless possession of the Dean and Chapter. Interestingly it had been loaned to the United States of America in 1939 for exhibition at the World's Fair in New York.

Below: The Queen stands with the civic dignitaries after unveiling the plaque to commemorate the official opening of the Pelham Bridge. The weather had not relented all through the visit but it did not deter the Queen or the Duke of Edinburgh nor did it dampen the enthusiasm of the crowds. It was remarked by a member of the royal entourage that this crowd was the biggest seen for some time to such a visit - a tribute indeed to the people of the city. After leaving the bridge, the Queen was driven to the Cathedral. There she unveiled a window in the Airmen's Chapel dedicated to the memory of those members of the Flying Training Command Units who gave their lives in the war. At the Usher Art Galley the Queen was very interested in the story of the building itself and, like the Prince of Wales some thirty years earlier, was particularly intrigued by the collection of watches. The visit to Lincoln came too quickly to an end as all royal visits do. The bridge that took so long to plan and build was now officially open. The Queen and Duke left for London by train. The large civic party left for lunch at the Saracen's Head and the people of Lincoln remembered a memorable day. As a postscript 20 years after that visit the commemorative plaque on the bridge was in such a poor condition, covered in dust, dirt, graffiti, posters and paint, that the inscription was illegible. Good thing a local businessman decided to clean it there and then.

A wet and bedraggled crowd gather at the Pelham Bridge awaiting the royal party. The official opening of the £650,000 bridge was a shorter than planned ceremony. The formal introductions were left until later when they were made at the Usher Gallery. Opening the bridge, the Queen said it was a bold and imaginative solution that was demanded if the city was to fulfil in the present day its function as the industrial, cultural and market centre of this part of England. One unfortunate result of the bad weather was that it marred the visit to Sincil Bank, home of Lincoln City AFC, to meet the schoolchildren of the city. Instead of dancing and singing on the field itself, the 11,000 children and their teachers had to remain in the stands. It did not stop them from cheering and yelling in excitement. As they waited for the royal party to arrive, they gave a passing passenger train the ROYAL TREATMENT. The Queen and the Duke, after meeting a selection of guests, including Bill Anderson, city's manager, and Miss N Gibson of Skellingthorpe Road Junior School, toured the ground in an open-topped Land Rover. They then mounted the Royal Box from where they heard a five minute interlude of music from the Lincoln City School Military Band.

The second musical interlude proved to be a thrill for the soloists, 11 year old Sandra Woodcock of Boultham Moor School and Mr E Spreabury, a member of St Mark's Church Choir. The cheering grew louder on the second tour of the ground. As the vehicle neared the exit, a spontaneous 'three cheers' resounded across the ground for the Royal visitors and naturally for the children themselves for having their planned activities curtailed because of the 'Queen's weather'. Even the dancing display by the children which was to have been held that evening had to be abandoned.

Wartime

'Welcome home' was the unanimous feeling as the volunteers of the Lincolnshire Companies returned on 16th May 1901 to Lincoln from the Boer War in South Africa. No effort had been spared to give these men a 'hearty and fitting welcome'. The Stonebow was decorated and tradesmen and shops were encouraged to follow suit. The soldiers reached Southampton at midday and a telegram announced they would reach Lincoln by the evening. At 6.30pm the Mayor greeted the company at the Great Northern Station yard opposite the Albion Hotel. They then marched to their barracks via St Mary's Street, High Street, Corporation Street, West Parade, Yarborough Road and Burton Road. A vast crowd had turned out in force to welcome the troops. The general feeling at the time was expressed by the Echo when it stated that all would 'warm to the patriotism' despite, it went on, what others say in the papers. Next day there was a banquet in the Drill Hall with the toast 'The Active Service Company' and once again the feeling of welcome was strongly expressed by a large crowd as it gathered outside. The sense of identity with local regiments and troops coupled with the national feeling for country and Empire was very strong. The sentiments expressed on this occasion would have been expected. Lincoln had given its troops a typical 'Welcome home'.

Bottom: The shadows of war were getting longer in 1938. Preparations for an eventual conflict seemed to have been a national preoccupation. Anderson shelters, civil defence, air raid wardens, evacuation, Red Cross - the list seemed endless. The fear of gas attack was very real. Thousands of ex-servicemen who had suffered from gas attacks in the First World War, the 'war to end all wars', were living reminders of their horrors. ARP volunteers were drilled in anti-gas measures, having to gingerly sniff tiny phials of the poisonous stuff to learn how to distinguish the distinctive odours of each type. It was serious. That is why Post Office workers in Lincoln, like everyone else in the country, were issued with gas masks as far back as 1937 and made to take part in special exercises. By September 1938 there had been 38 million gas masks issued to men, women and children in Britain. Children took quite happily to the special 'Mickey Mouse' gas mask designed to give this macabre precaution the appearance of a game. A 'gas-helmet' was issued to babies. There was even a gas-proof pram invented by a nurseryman from Kent. The London, Midland and Scottish Railway experimented with an anti-gas train. However disagreeable it was to try on a gas mask for the first time, it did bring home to people the grim reality of the approaching war.

Right: Films and footage of the major wars of this century will generally show a high powered tank thundering across a terrain giving the appearance of being indestructible. Then we are bought up short when there is footage of tanks taking part in the first world war and realise by today's standards how destructible they appeared then. But they had just come into service. It is said that their introduction was the turning point of the war. The origins of the tank lay in Lincoln, the 'home of the tank' as it is termed now. Originally they were called landships, made at Foster and company in the city. The first in 1914 was almost a modified tractor, the brains behind it being Mr William Tritton, then the firm's managing director. By 1915 Fosters had been given the entire responsibility for the tanks' production. Foster's works became a 'highly driven dynamo' building 'Little Willie' then 'Big Willie' a year later. This new weapon of war was given the name 'tank' by the workmen who originally worked on it. The tank's first appearance was at the Battle of the Somme in 1916. It was not a success. The heavy machines were bogged down in the mud. It was not until they performed on dry ground at Cambrai that the tanks showed how effective they could be. What the introduction of the tank did do was ensure that there was work in Foster's Foundry for male and female employees alike, all being employed on the production line. There is a sort of mark of the macabre in the skull and crossbones seen here with some of the workers with their tank.

The bombs that exploded on that fateful night in January 1943 caused damage to lives and property. The bombs that did not explode caused heartache and fear to those whose homes and businesses were near. Here we see the experts from the Royal Engineers led by Captain Price looking nonchalantly pleased with themselves after they had defused an unexploded bomb from Meltons printers some time later. Meltons was situated in St Benedict's Square behind Marks and Spencers and Binks's the bicycle shop. This 1000lb bomb had penetrated the roof, the first floor, ground floor and then buried itself 24 feet down in soft sand on the edge of the River Whitham. Goodness knows would have happened if it had have gone off. On this occasion businesses in the city centre were closed until it was made safe and that was not until 12 days later. It is hard to imagine having to wait nearly two weeks not knowing if or when this thing would wreak havoc. It was later discovered that the bomb had fallen very close to the river wall, next not only to a main sewer but also to a 750 line telephone cable. Imagine the differing kinds of chaos that could have produced. Fortunately the only damage was to the printers and the wall. Could have been worse!

> **THE BOMBS THAT RAINED DOWN ON LINCOLN IN JANUARY 1943 CAUSED UNTOLD DAMAGE TO LIVES AND PROPERTY**

Above: That fateful raid by the German bomber did cause damage and fatalities and injuries. Dixon Street was very badly affected. The bomb that fell outside numbers 3 and 15 did explode. Fortunately no-one was killed but two men fell into the crater, one being pinned down by a coping stone which had fallen from a house. Again, fortunately, his injuries were minor. The residents at the time of the raid were in their Morrison shelter. There were other casualties as a result of this single raid. An air raid warden was killed in Avondale Street. There were four deaths altogether, 30 people were injured and serious damage to property was caused. Those of us who have never had to experience this sort of thing find it hard to imagine the terror felt when the air raid warning sounded. Then the drone of the plane, the bombs exploding, the damage, the uncertainty. How was anyone to know how many planes there were on this particular raid? How many bombs would be dropped? Where and how were your family and friends? Was it to be your house next? Would there be further raids? Fear of danger is often a worse nightmare.

Right: The lone German bomber raid on that January night in 1943 caused much distress

through just through the unexploded bombs. Here in Thomas Street it was not until the Sunday morning that a bomb that had landed in the middle of the street went off. The impact was even felt by a lady as she was putting her six children into the Morrison shelter. She described later how she felt the movement of the earth through the floor. A gentleman who had just finished delivering meat for Handley's butchers shop in Sincil Street had just parked his van in a garage at the top of Thomas Street. As he rode away on his bicycle, the force of the bomb falling on to the road knocked him to the ground. The bomb was immediately sandbagged and all the nearby houses were evacuated. Now was the time to be worried. Would it explode? If so, when? What would happen to the house?

That fateful day, a Sunday, it went off in the early hours of the morning. The damage to this narrow street was devastating. Houses 5 to 17 and 10 to 26 were destroyed. After the war 17 houses had to be rebuilt and several which had been badly damaged were repaired. All because of one plane. Soon after the raid it was shot down but not before it had cause distress and devastation to the people and city of Lincoln.

The evening of 15th January 1943 was a normal war-time evening for Lincoln. The voluntary organisations were as usual going about their tasks, servicemen and women were again relaxing in the city. Then a solitary German bomber flew over the city and dropped high explosive, incendiary and phosphorous bombs. The training which the ARP, the Home Guard, WVS and Ambulance personnel had undergone was now put to the test. Here we see the result of the raid in Vernon Street, off High Street. The shed at Number 1 received a direct hit. The bomb for some reason failed to explode and, as the family had gone out, the only casualty was the dog. ARP wardens soon realised there was an unexploded bomb threatening the lives of the street's residents. They were quickly evacuated to either relatives or to a nearby rest centre. The bomb could not be defused and at 11pm it went off. The Clark house at 1 Vernon Street was completely destroyed and shops which backed on to the street were damaged. The family at Number 1 had lost their home. If there was any consolation, and war does not bring many, it was that the house was empty and the bomb did not explode on impact so everyone in the area was able to get out. Mr Clarke was on his way home from work at the time, his wife had gone to stay with a neighbour and their daughter, Audrey, was helping out at the forces' canteen at the Hannah Chapel. Like most tragedies in war time this was a small part of a very large picture but a major part of the lives of the people who are most affected.

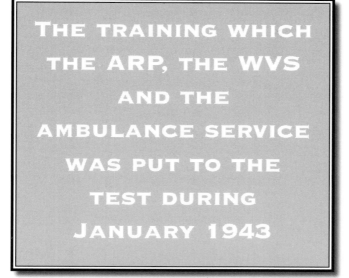

THE TRAINING WHICH THE ARP, THE WVS AND THE AMBULANCE SERVICE WAS PUT TO THE TEST DURING JANUARY 1943

Above: The end of the war in Europe brought a national thanksgiving. Villages, towns and cities throughout the land were quick to ensure that this should be celebrated in an appropriate manner. Lincoln held its services on 13th May 1945. Here we see the members of the Women's Land Army, part of the great parade after the service in the Cathedral. The contribution of the Land Army to Britain's war effort was immense. Before the war this country imported 60% of its food; hostilities meant that we needed to produce our own. The Land Army, a feature in the 1914-18 War, was re-introduced. 'Army' was a something of a misnomer. There was a uniform of green jersey, brown breeches, brown felt slouch hat and khaki overcoat, often modified to suit personal taste. The members had often to work where they were sent; they were denied the official use of forces' canteens in whatever leisure time they had. They were entitled to seven days' leave a year and frequently had to pay their own fare home out of the meagre wages they were given. The Ministry of Information portrayed them as bursting with vitality and bathed in permanent sunshine - the reality was somewhat different. It is worth noting that, in spite of the back-breaking toil of the work, the drop out rate was lower than in industry. It often took time for the women to be accepted. A Lincolnshire land girl reported one incident, after she collided with a farm worker, thus: 'Cum art road, yer gaupin' b....r' said Alec. The other men turned round in horror. Then, seeing I was laughing and not flat on the floor in a swoon, they joyously received the word back into their

vocabularies. ....From that moment on I began to belong to the farm. I became 'Owd yaller 'ead', 'Sparrer', 'gaupie' or 'oo' (she).'

Right: There had been two services of thanksgiving that day, an afternoon one for civilians and an evening service, followed by a parade through the city. This was to remember the contribution that the Armed Forces, the Auxiliary Services and the Civil Defence had made. The huge crowds who gathered that day to give thanks that war was over had waited outside the Cathedral for over two hours, some trying to scale the drainpipes to obtain a better view. Three thousand men and women took part in this service and parade. The Armed Forces, particularly the RAF and Women's Auxiliary Air Force, had pride of place. There was for the auxiliary forces a spot in the city's gratitude. Lincoln saw on parade members of the National and Auxiliary Fire Service, the Women's Land Army, the Auxiliary Territorial Service, Red Cross, St John's Ambulance, Fire Guard, Home Guard, Royal Observer Corps, Women's Voluntary Service, Army and Sea Cadets, the ATC and the Girl's Training Corps. In 1939 millions of women had joined these and other organisations to serve their country. First Aid, helping with evacuees, nursing, providing shelter and food, becoming the backbone of help to the civilian and military population. They worked on the land, in factories, in schools, in hospitals. The city and the nation gave thanks in the most appropriate way it could to all those people who had made VE day possible.

Above: Savings became a national obsession in the second world war. Drives included War Weapons Weeks, Warship Week, Wings for Victory and Salute The Soldiers. Slogans were everywhere, part of the everyday scene. 'Don't Take The Squander Bug when You Go Shopping' was one typical as the country was advised, encouraged and often told what to do. Posters were on hoardings, at all places where the public would gather and as we can see here on this Lincoln bus on every aspect of public transport. By 1943 the average citizen was saving up to a quarter of his or her disposable income, not least because there were so few goods to spend it on. Children were encouraged to take part. Schools had a weekly Savings Day.

> **DURING WORLD WAR II, THE COUNTRY WAS ADVISED, ENCOURAGED AND OFTEN *TOLD* WHAT TO DO**

You would take your 6d to the teacher and she would give you a 6d stamp. These stamps bore the slogan 'Defend the Right to be Free'. Thirty of these bought a 15s National Savings Certificate with a promised value of £1. 0s. 6d. after ten years. Another type of saving encouraged involved material things. 'We Want Your Kitchen Waste' was a poster showing a cheerful pig exhorting us to save. There were paper-drives. At least 100 tons of paper were needed to build a battleship; six old books provided enough material for one mortar shell carrier. And so it went on - campaign after campaign, slogan after slogan. And they worked.

Changing city

A forlorn sight and the end of an era as the Hannah Memorial Wesleyan Chapel at the corner of High Street and Chaplin Street is demolished. There is still a chance for the gentleman to admire for the last time the imposing frontage in Italian classic character and just about recall the six columns surrounded by a cornice with wings on either side. Or perhaps he is just giving instructions to the man on the first floor what to destroy next. The chapel had been closed in 1962 after serving the local Methodist community since 1875. During the height of the second world war it had acted as a forces' canteen. It could seat 1000 people and as well as its architecture it was also remembered for the magnificent organ. Its congregation moved across the road to Portland Place Central Methodist Chapel. That was replaced too by the new Central Methodist Chapel, the old building being formerly in St Benedict's Square until Marks and Spencer needed to extend its premises. The new chapel, built at a cost of £150,000, has the appearance of a modern building, nothing at all like the Hannah Memorial.

Oxford Street looking towards the Durham Ox and the footbridge over the railway before the work started on the new Pelham Bridge. Work began in 1956 and led to the demolition of nearly fifty houses, nineteen shops, two garages and a pub. The close knit area around Melville Street made way for the northern end and the whole outlook of the city was to be transformed. The debate about crossings and bridges and demolition was a fierce one at times and led to a great deal of frustration. The debate as to the bridge's name was conducted in a civilised fashion and threw up some interesting suggestions. Lindum was a favourite,

Cathedral Approach for obvious reasons was another, as was Minster, St Andrews and Oxhill, 'Ox' for Oxford Street and 'Hill' after the Chairman of the council's Level Crossings Committee, Alderman Hill. Ruston was another choice while a local newspaper correspondent suggested, appropriately it might seem considering what function this new structure was going to perform, Stoparc - Solving Temporarily Our Problems Against Level Crossings. But whatever the debate about its name, the need for it was agreed in order to keep the flow of traffic moving as it was continually being held up by trains crossing.

The Durham Ox Hotel overlooked the level crossing between the railway sheds and the station and as we look towards the market area of the city we can see a sight repeated many times over during the day - cars and buses and pedestrians waiting for the train to pass. Further along are the premises of Gilberts, the motor distributors. Try to imagine what would have happened if the bridge had not been built - look at the hold ups caused today at the southern end of High Street near Wigford Way. The disruption that this crossing caused was enormous. Traffic coming from Melville Street and Oxford Street met here. It was not until October 1959 that the Durham Ox crossing went and then there were

protests from the residents of Canwick Street and
Northern Terrace but then nothing could save it. In
the two years it took to build the bridge there was
still rail traffic to contend with and the area between
the LMS and LNER tracks proved to be a very
difficult problem. No delays to trains were to be
tolerated and a minimum of six feet clearance of all
running lines had to be maintained at all times. The
entire signalling system was moved, track rods and
switches re-positioned, telephone wires and poles
dismantled and run underground and an electrified
signal system installed. No problems to the
engineers you would think. And a more modern
railtrack thrown in as well.

The building of the bridge meant there were many casualties and among them were the premises of Gilbert and Sons Ltd. The firm was established in 1876 as a sewing machine and washing machine dealer but by 1936 was a prominent motor distributor. Looking at the photograph there are names there which remind us of the days when we had British cars - Morris, Wolseley, especially its 'better class' mini, the Hornet and its counterpart the Riley Elf. Gilberts occupied a temporary building after leaving here and moved to a permanent site in 1961 near the Pelham Bridge itself. The firm closed down in 1981 after 105 years in Lincoln. Other well established businesses to suffer were the wood turners, Ruston and Dawkins, Halls Brush Makers and the fishing tackle dealers S A Nobbs and Son. These were concentrated in Norman Street and with them went several private houses. The whole area was to be transformed. There were questions in Parliament not about whether the scheme was worthwhile but when it would start. The project was announced in July 1954 and would be the biggest in the city since the new power station 14 years earlier. But in October 1955 the local, MP Mr Geoffrey de Freitas, had to ask the Minister of Transport if the building of the bridge was being slowed down because of budget cuts - things don't change much. There was no reason for any delay, was the ministerial reply. So work was begun in the following year.

> ## GILBERT & SONS WAS ESTABLISHED IN 1876 AS A SEWING MACHINE AND WASHING MACHINE DEALER

Below: Canwick Road stands now almost in the shadow of the southern end of the bridge beside the rail lines. But change is inevitable for any city or town and streets and people are always affected. The houses on Canwick Road at the time of the building of the Pelham Bridge were built in the nineteenth century like many of the houses in the St Andrews area of the city. They originally housed workers employed at the nearby engineering works of Robert Robey and Company who built 200 houses in the area. Consider now the changes which have taken place since the construction of the bridge. The need for the bridge was to avoid the congestion caused by the level crossings. Most towns and cities are thankful for only one main line station. Lincoln had two because of the nineteenth century rivalry between two railway companies who

built stations on the High Street. This resulted in two crossings there until as late as 1985. As a result of the coming of the Great Northern loop line, trains at one time travelled out of these stations in seven directions. The tracks and sidings occupied a large area and Lincoln had to cope with that - and in the middle of the city as well.

Bottom: Whenever there is work going on there will always be an interested if not critical group of spectators keeping a very watchful eye on things. The conversation would also run to trying to remember what was there before it all began. What seemed a large area at one time now appears very small as you recall what was previously there. One of the first problems that had to be faced by the bridge builders was that a culvert had to be constructed over the Sincil Dyke for the then Lincolnshire River Board. This was then decked over to provide for further development on the west side of the bridge and for car parking by Ruston and Hornsby on the other. Even before that was underway a test trial hole was dug. The problems of water and sand meant that the area here had to be drained and secured so that any outside water could not penetrate. That allowed machines needed for excavation to be used. The sand and silt which had to be replaced by a more compact bed would not take the weight of a man let alone a machine. All very compli-cated and all very necessary.

Above: One of the survivors of the onslaught on the area was the Crown and Cushion at the corner of Melville Street and Newton Street. The streets however are showing the signs of tear but maybe not wear. Melville Street itself was soon to be transformed into the city's main road as greatness was thrust upon it, at the expense of getting rid of all the slum properties around it. They would have gone anyway no matter whether a bridge was being built or not. One very interesting part of the city was to suffer and that was the old Victoria Bridge, constructed in 1843 and had carried traffic all that time. It was found to be in good condition in spite of the increase in number of vehicles and size of loads over the years. Fortunately, the heavy traffic had not caused any damage - even the pitch-pine piles it had been built on were in a perfect state of preservation. A brick arch tapering from four feet thick to fourteen inches thick at the crown. A tribute to the engineers and craftsmen of the nineteenth century.

Below: Work at last underway on the Pelham Bridge. Like all such work it brings a great deal of inconvenience. That lady is finding it difficult to manoeuvre the pram outside the Oxford Hotel. Traffic is slowed and trade in the Oxford Hotel was slowed as well. It appears access to it was the equivalent of a steeplechase. The problem of the culvert was the chief cause of this disruption. It was 450 feet long, 35 feet wide and 12 feet deep and all because of the nature of the land which made the excavation for the bridge's foundations virtually impossible without this work. It was said that the planning for this operation took longer than it did to build the bridge, a test of the ingenuity and skill of the engineers involved. What we take for granted in any construction is usually because someone has sorted the problems out beforehand. In a huge scale project as this those problems had to be solved They were so complicated that the two years it did take in the planning was necessary for obviously the foundations of this bridge had to be secure. That matters not probably to this lady though. All she wants is a safe passage now.

Looking at the part completed bridge it is easy to appreciate that it should be named after the Cathedral for the view from the south now of Lincoln's famous landmark is magnificent. It now matches the views that can seen from all other angles. The building of this bridge was to the people of the city a little like going to the dentist or having to take medicine when you were a child. It caused a shudder or two at first but the effect was usually wonderful. The treatment Lincoln had to undergo was the equivalent of several fillings often without being numbed first. Roads were closed, traffic was diverted, sewers, surface water drains, gas mains, electricity cables and telephone cables either were re-routed or re-laid. No treatment ever goes

DURING THE BUILDING OF THE BRIDGE ROADS WERE CLOSED, TRAFFIC DIVERTED AND CABLES AND WATERMAINS RE-ROUTED

smoothly. On one occasion the main feeder cable to Ruston's Works was missed by the piletube cutting edge by only two inches because the cable was not where the plans said it should have been. Think of the chaos that would have caused if the worst had happened. British Railways, as then called, allowed possession of the tracks for only five nights from 11.30pm to 5am. Fortunately the work was carried out smoothly and accurately. What was also very interesting as we look at this photograph is that the council decided that a large site to the north of Norman Street should be kept clear in anticipation of its consideration for the erection there of a Civic Centre.

On the move

The first double-decker bus to go through Stonebow on to High Street in September 1927. The view is looking north at the no.5 bus to St Giles. The bus is a Leyland reg TD 9522. A small crowd has gathered and like the policeman near Saltergate and the one on point duty they are just as interested in the cameraman. But why such an interest in this bus? The probable answer was that this was a trial demonstration of a Titan double decker bus, the first to come to Lincolnshire, let alone pass under the city's Stonebow. It all took place on a very quiet Sunday morning and whether those responsible ever considered putting Stonebow on the 'double-decker' bus route is not clear. A bit of a tight fit then and the driver would always need a steady nerve. Another interesting fact about this occasion was that it was considered important enough for this scene not only to be commemorated on film but also as a work of art. A painting of it at one time hung in the transport office at the depot in St Mark's, Lincoln. Obviously in many people's eyes a very significant occasion.

The city's first bus service was inaugurated in 1920 and from then on the service grew as the city itself expanded. The buses could go where the trams could not reach but there were problems. The early vehicles had solid rubber tyres and wooden seats and with the quality of the road surfaces being then not what we expect today passengers had a very uncomfortable journey. The buses were still a popular and often the only means of transport. Standards did improve particularly when the city introduced these Leyland 'Titan' double-deckers, a later edition pictured here in the 1940s in the St Mark's Street garage which had been opened in November 1928. A trial was held to see whether they would get under the Stonebow Arch. It was successful and this meant that the tram system could be abandoned; buses could do the job better. Towns and cities before and after the war took great pride in running their own transport system. It almost became a matter of rivalry with other towns that their buses were more punctual, quicker, more comfortable than the neighbours. But Lincoln had a problem; it was very difficult to make a real profit, mainly because of its size and shape as well because of the competition. The narrow city streets and the north-south shape of the city limited a great deal of transport activity. There were not the massive housing developments outside the city centre that other places had. Once out of the city centre there were villages rather than estates. The corporation also presumably could only operate within the city boundary. Other companies competed for those services and there were many of them. Cars also became a more convenient way to travel into and out of the city. Hence the building of Pelham Bridge, Wigford Way and the Western by-pass.

Above: A double decker bus manoeuvres its way through the archway of the Stonebow towards Battle's Corner past the solitary shopper. In the background are the tops of three landmarks in the city. There is the tower of the church of St Mary-le-Wigford and Mammon represented by Lloyds and the Midland Banks. This photograph was taken from scaffolding around the front of Mawer and Collingham. What can just be seen from this unusual view is the distinctive frontage of the store. It became Binns, part of the House of Fraser group in 1980; now it is just the House of Fraser. But compare what you see in the photograph of the old store and what is there now - a controversial change indeed! It is interesting that Lincoln City was supposed to have played its first matches near here before moving to Sincil Bank in 1884. The Guidhall itself has, under the aegis of the local trust, been restored and retains much of the grandeur of its past 800 years or more. The Lincoln guide book says 'layer and layer of History' when talking about the city and the Guildhall is just that.

Above: This very striking and controversial building on Brayford Wharf after its redevelopment in 1959 was built for The Lincolnshire Motor Company. Apart from being concrete the most interesting aspect of it was the roof, described as 'hyperbolic paraboloid' in form. A dictionary definition only confuses it even more so it is best left to be said that it was a potential game winner at Scrabble and the largest and one of the first examples in the country. The company was the main dealer for Ford cars, tractors and commercial vehicles. However in 1971 the building, known as Brayford House, was entirely re-modelled to house the Lindsey and Holland County Library which subsequently became the headquarters of the Lincolnshire Library Service. The reason for this upheaval was that the former Newland suite was cramped and inadequate, particularly in storage space. Books were spread into many different rooms, difficult to get at and often collections were separated. The staff worked under great difficulty in 16 small rooms and in two houses with three floors. The massive increase in the public's desire for books of all kinds, for learning and for reference, meant that the facilities had to be centralised and adequate. This garage, despite the pits, but with the roof, was considered a most suitable replacement.

Right: Saltergate Garage at the entrance to the one-way system of Saltergate itself. The garage has had to make way for the redevelopment of the area. At first glance today it appears on the outside that very little else has changed or as is said in another context the street has 'kept its shape'. The secret of any redevelopment it is said is that there should be little or no change to the way a building or a street looks unless there is an obvious need, such as in slum clearance. Often, especially in the schemes which took place in the 1960s and 70s, there was a lack of sensitivity about many of them. We need the past to learn for the future. The Chinese saw it as a reservoir of human experience. To have placed into a city centre buildings and schemes which are totally out of character with what is there already is an intrusion. The Waterside Centre from Saltergate does not appear to have changed the street's appearance. There seems to have been this regard for the keeping of what is acceptable and good. The centre itself has its own distinctive style and character. At some future date when it has outlived its usefulness and been replaced by something more in keeping with those times, people will look back at it with the same kind of nostalgia as often we do today at things that are lost.

THE LIBRARY WAS EQUIPPED WITH MOBILE SHELVES, HOUSING ABOUT 40,000 VOLUMES

Now instead of mechanics, pits, petrol pumps and ramps and Novasealing equipment and Ford cars, one with a very interesting registration number, there were to be in Brayford House thousands of books. This new library was opened in March 1971 by Alderman J E Sandars, who also opened the premises as a garage in 1959. The library was not to be a lending library like the one in Free School Lane. The books were collections of materials such as music, drama, foreign books, local government and education. There was a separate room for books on Lincolnshire - a massive reference collection to treasure. To house these books the library was equipped with mobile shelves, housing about 40,000 volumes. The shelves each contained 1,000 books and were designed so that they could be easily slid on runners, a bit heavy for the poor library assistants nonetheless. But after the cramped conditions under which they had to operate at Newland, the new premises at Brayford House, with its hyperbolic paraboloid roof, would be nothing other than a welcome replacement and for the researcher a boon.

What an asset Brayford Pool has been to Lincoln and in many ways still is. Brayford at one time was a busy port and as we can see in this 1968 view looking towards East Wharf there is much evidence of this then. It was surrounded by warehouses and boat yards but we can see evidence here that the 'modernisation' of the area has begun to take place and not to everyone's liking. There are the reminders here of the great days of the Pool, of trade, of river traffic and the hustle and bustle of it all. The north side still retains much of this while on the south side towards Holmes's the evidence lies in the water and the stillness of the buildings alongside. It would be inevitable that Brayford would decline as a port as it was following the national trend. There would then be an opportunity to retain that atmosphere which the architecture at least provided. The mills and warehouses we see here have almost all gone. An example must be Hercocks in the top corner of this photograph which was demolished despite being considered worth preserving. A pity for the replacements are not unique; you can see the like in any urban re-development in this country. Brayford and Lincoln had something unique here.

Shopping spree

The construction of Wigford Way in 1971 as part of an inner ring road scheme was the city's answer to the problem of the vast increase in traffic at that time. Pelham Bridge was an earlier attempt to tackle the problem; this was the next. What the construction did do was to deprive Lincoln of some very interesting buildings, including the a mid-Georgian block between 183 and 187 High Street. As well as the architecture, it must have had a very interesting history. The whole block was once a large town house but by the end of the nineteenth century had been split into shops and a hotel, this being number 185, the Waverley Hotel. The interior of the building showed how grand the original house must

have been for the finely decorated ceilings remained until the building was demolished. Planners have very difficult decisions to make when projects like Wigford Way are to be carried out. The need for an effective transportation system has to be balanced with a need to preserve what is an integral part of the city. On this occasion this block of property did not survive. It may well be that if the scheme was put forward today, there might have been ways of retaining a building of such interest and significance as well as addressing the more modern demands of traffic and road systems. These days there is probably a greater sensitivity to these issues than there was 20 or more years ago.

Right: Liptons was presumably one the first supermarkets in Lincoln when it opened in the High Street in the early 1960s, vying with Mason's for the shoppers' custom. This was the time when the streets of our towns began to see national shops and stores take over from locally owned ones which for years had been a feature of the locality. Times were changing. According to the Prime Minister at the time, Harold McMillan, we had 'never had it so good'. The demand for goods was changing. What were once considered luxuries were then regarded as essentials. Colour televisions, refrigerators and washing machines became normal things to possess the same way as in the early 1990s we sought video recorders, deep freezers and computers. The same applied to food shops, to fashion and clothing shops. We became consumers and suddenly the emphasis began to change. The consumer dictated demand. Nationally owned shops realised this and had the resources to meet the change. This impact of national chains began to tell but many local shops fought on. Some still survive in the city. It is interesting that even shops like Liptons found life difficult. They, Maypole. Home and Colonial and lesser names like Broughs and Meadows did what other companies in other businesses did. They became one, called the Home and Colonial Group while still retaining their names and individual shop fronts. There is not much individuality about High Street Liptons in 1964, however.

Below: A corner of High Street and St Mary's Street in 1963 at what was known as Halford's Corner. The church of St Mary-le Wigford and the Queens Hotel can be made out but a lot of what can be seen here has gone to make way for Wigford Way. Halfords had been on this site since 1910 but had undergone some rebuilding and extension since then. To make space for Wigford Way Lincoln lost many of its well known shops and businesses, including the Albion, one of the city's best known hotels and later a public house. The whole of the property on the west side of the High Street was to be demolished to make way for this development in 1970-71. Some of the buildings to be lost were part of the city's architectural heritage. But the need to accommodate the increase in traffic in the area, particularly with the new Pelham Bridge allowing greater access into and out of the city, meant there had to be some kind of 'vehicular relief'. It is often the case that a scheme to improve traffic flow only partly solves the problem; all it usually means is the number of vehicles using it rises and the problem still remains. What Lincoln got here was the beginning of pedestrianisation, a subway and the High Street cut into two. Part solving of the traffic problem but at what cost to the city itself?

A 1972 photograph of the Covered Market. The secret of its success and that of any other market is the combination of a range of goods rather like a supermarket combined with the informality and personal service of a small local shop. Lose those and you end up with a glorified shopping mall and today there are enough of those about. The history of Lincoln's markets is one of regular redevelopment, inevitable as the city itself changed and developed. The one thing however that the market tried to retain in the 1970s was, as one of its stall-holders termed it, 'the old world charm of shopping'. A typical example at about this time was the family tradition of traders, especially those who brought thousands of eggs, fruit and flowers,

vegetables and preserves to the market every Friday. Some had been known to have been coming to Lincoln for over 50 years. Among those at this time were Amy Hetherington and her sisters and cousins, Elsie Gash, Brenda Pacey and Mildred Hewitt. One of the better known figures was 'Auntie Betsy' who was still making and selling her jam, marmalade and lemon curd at the age of 74 years. Her real name was Betsy Proctor, a market trader for over 40 years. She had taken over the stall from her mother. That is a small example of the people who carried on the market tradition in Lincoln; there were others with their own specialities to sell. That is what gives a market its unique atmosphere in any town and city.

At work

Below: The typhoid epidemic of 1905 in Lincoln had been a profound shock to the city. The Lincoln tap water had been polluted by sewerage entering the River Whitham and adjacent streams with pollution affecting Hartsholme Lake and Boultham Ballast Pits. By April of that year there were 900 reported cases in the city and by then there were over 100 deaths. Afterwards Lincoln sought to ensure there should be no repetition of this disaster. Water was to be piped in from Elkesley in Nottinghamshire and work began on that in 1908. By a feat of engineering which was a marvel at the time Lincoln had a scheme which would ensure clean water for its citizens. The disruption to the city was worth it as water mains were laid throughout the length and breadth of the city. Here we see the work at the top of High Street as the scheme, which cost over £248,000, was nearing completion. The other cost was in terms of people's lives a few years earlier. That newspaper headline of 3rd February 1911 looks interesting. Peter the Painter, alias Peter Piatkow, was the reputed leader of a group of anarchists who held out against 40 policemen, a platoon of the Scots Guards, the Fire Brigade and a detachment of Royal Engineers for six hours in the famous Siege of Sidney Street in the East End of London.

Right: It is not often that you see a serving policeman used as a real life model advertising a company's products. This is what is happening here to PC 30 Keith S Dixon of the local force in 1960. The motor cycle is a 500cc Triumph registration number NVL 766 and here he is outside the Judgment Porch of Lincoln Cathedral displaying the machine and the new 2-way radio. What the Triumph Motor Cycle Company did was to use this photograph in its advertising. The Speed Twin, because of its reliability, was the standard machine of the Metropolitan Police Force and other forces followed suit. The police machines were the standard bearer for Triumph although the management did complain that very little money was made from them as the production run had to be regularly altered as each regional force wanted the 500 built to its own specifications. The two-way radio-telephone demonstrated here was built in the mid 1960s by a firm in Wembley. It was tried out by the Metropolitan force and proved capable of covering the force's area. Presumably what that force did today, other forces did the next. This was worth publicising in a massive endorsement of the Triumphs and hence this photograph to do just that.

Patients, nurses and a couple of visitors pose for this photograph taken in 1958 in Digby ward of St George's Hospital. Everyone looks as content as you can be in a hospital but what a struggle to get things moving here after the war. The keys to the hospital were handed over to Mr Eric Scorer, Chairman of Lincoln Hospital Committee, in 1948 from the Army authorities as during the war it had been a military hospital. The hospital had five acres of buildings spread over a 15 acre site with accommodation for 600 civilian patients. What it did not have however was plaster on the walls for one thing. It would take at least a year to bring it up to standard. An operating theatre and X-ray department were priorities. Decisions had to be made as to whether there would be an out-patients department and what other medical services would be provided. From today's viewpoint it seems astonishing that there should have been such a debate. This makes you wonder what kind of treatment patients received during the war. As this 1958 photograph shows, things have obviously improved in the time since it was opened.

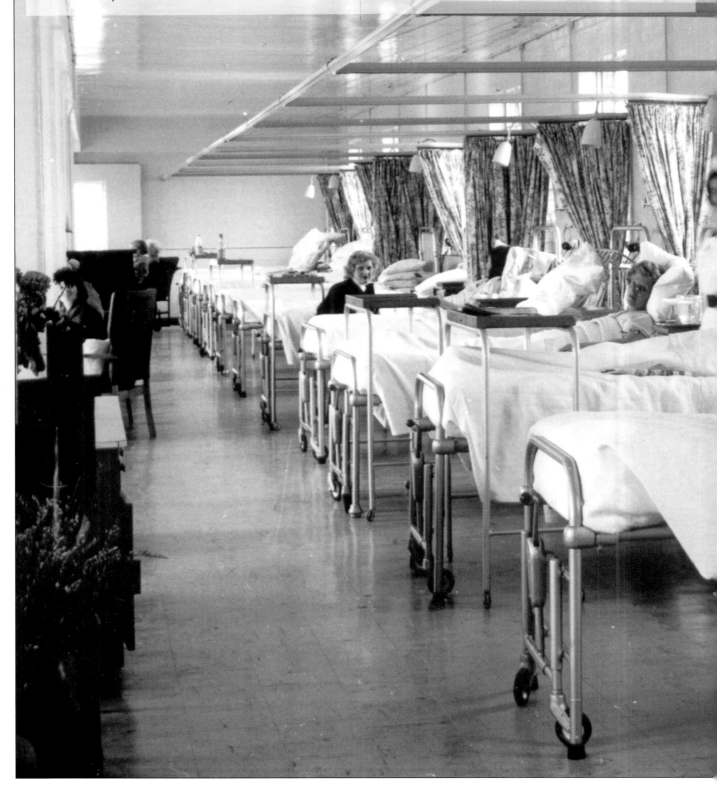

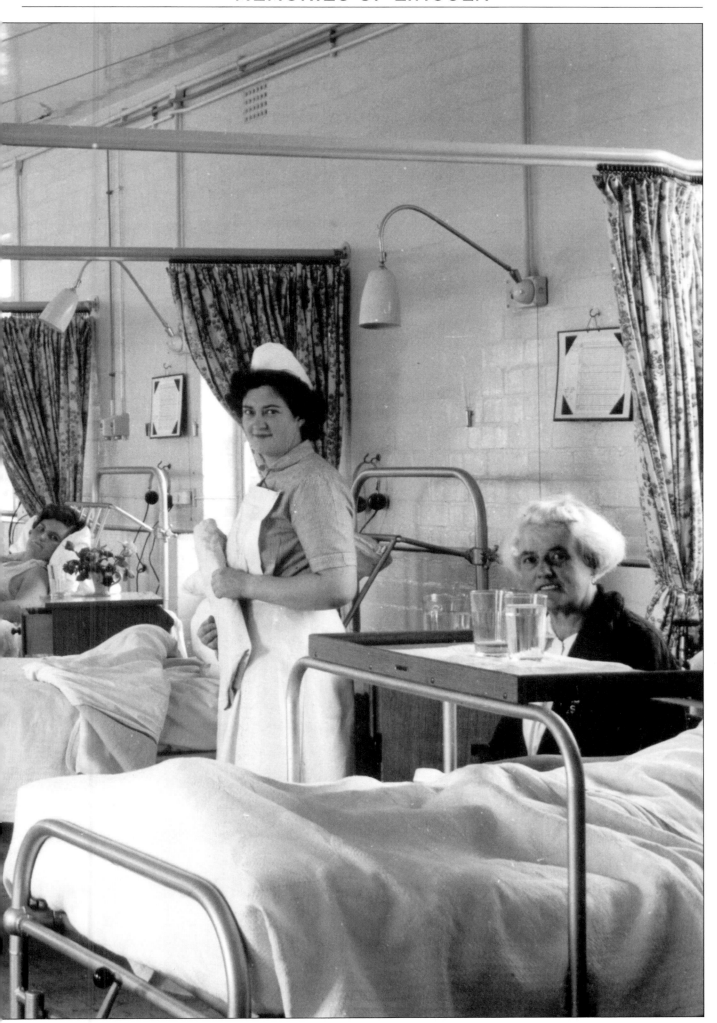

The visit of Edward, Prince of Wales to Lincoln in May 1927 was typical of many royal visits. Tightly scheduled and all packed into a short period of time. The Prince, according to a local newspaper report at the time, enjoyed this visit to the works of Rustons more than any other part of his visit. The paper stated 'It was appropriate that the Royal Ambassador of Europe should visit the homes of those mighty engines which played so large a part in the Empire's development'. The Prince does seem quite at home having the mechanics of the crane explained to him. This was not the main reason for the Royal visit. That was to officially open the new Usher Art Gallery. Wherever he went, he was met by large crowds wildly cheering this very popular young man.

He had laid a wreath at the city's War Memorial with local members of TOC H. He was greeted by 3,000 schoolchildren at the Arboretum. There he met children whose fathers had died in the First World War, with a special greeting for little Florrie Tingle who had been chosen to represent them. His other engagements appropriately were at the Cathedral with a special service held at the Soldiers' Memorial Chapel and a visit to the Old Palace. Lunch with the Mayor was held at the White Hart Hotel, He visited the St Giles Estate and then on to Rustons. After inspecting the crane the Prince had tea in the works canteen before catching the royal train home to London. Quite a hectic day for the royal visitor and a memorable one for Lincoln.

The house that Jack built

Jackson's Hardware Ltd was started by Eric Jackson on 15 July 1946 using his 'Demob Grant' for capital. He then employed two assistants in his street corner ironmongers shop in the High Street. As the business grew he was joined by Barry, his first son, in 1948, and two years later by his second son David. It was in these early years that Eric Jackson determined that trading primarily as a builders merchant was the way to achieve the most satisfactory turnover.

In 1952 the first of his innovatory plans took off in the form of his Jackard Fireplaces which offered a choice of household fireplaces to domestic customers in an era when the majority of homes were heated by solid fuel fires. Central heating was virtually limited to institutions and public buildings and few householders aspired to the expensive dreams of central heating as shown in films and glossy magazines.

The first of sixteen branches was opened in 1955 in the small market town of Spilsby, in the Wolds, its small population of 3,000 was swelled on market days by a regular influx of shoppers from the rural hinterland. They were catered for by Jacksons

having showroom space to display the latest in fitted kitchens, bathroom suites and boilers at a time when the new concept of planned kitchens was bathed in a romantic glow. By comparison this was a time when independent owner/driver bus operators making only the one return journey would while

Above: The original High Street premises. Below: An interior view of the High Street store taken in the early 1950s.

Above: *From left to right; Barry Jackson, the current Chairman, his father Eric, the Company founder and his brother David, pictured in the 1960s.*

away the Saturday afternoons doing the shopping for cottagers and farm wives too busy to make the journey themselves.

In 1959 when the growing company opened its second branch in the town of Newark-on-Trent in Nottinghamshire its payroll had risen to seventy-five. The premises containing shop, showroom and office block had sufficient space for builders and plumbers materials. For three shops to gross a turnover of £418,000 in the late fifties was good going indeed at a time when National Service men in the Forces were paid around £2 a week all found and young shop assistants were not much better off.

The same year saw the carefully planned refurbishment of the High Street parent shop completed and Eric Jackson, after little more than twelve years in charge of his own business, was honoured by being elected as President of the National Federation of Ironmongers.

This institution, now called the British Hardware Federation, works to protect the interests of, and to maintain standards in, a trade which for generations was run by family businesses with one of the heaviest outlays in stock in trade found in any High Street.

The ambition to expand as trade warranted such progress was continued by the family opening a branch in Grantham, a growing industrial town then catering for a market gardening and farming

countryside, in 1962. This branch dealt almost exclusively with builders and plumbers requisites and soon after the branch was able to expand into adjoining premises to provide warehouse facilities as well as the normal shop, offices and showroom. It was followed six years later by the fifth branch in Scunthorpe, a major centre of the UK's Steel manufacturing trade.

In 1968 the Jacksons also made another decisive move in taking over the rival company of Shipley and Co Ltd which had shops in Lincoln, Brigg and Gainsborough. Having done so the family took a cool hard look at what they had achieved, where they were and where they intended going. It was time for rationalising the management of their stock, their outlets, and concentrating on the areas and customers where they saw the best opportunities.

As a result of the amalgamation the new enterprise combined names when it moved to new headquarters at Pelham House in 1971 under the banner of Jackson Shipley Ltd. These had been part of the former Robey Works in Canwick Road and provided much needed space.

The larger organisation with a turnover of £2,780,000 enjoyed greater purchasing power with its suppliers, including nationally famed companies such as Aga, Ideal Standard and Hepworth and the larger manufacturers supplying the full range of building and plumbing materials. The company was then employing 230 people some thirty five years after starting with two shop assistants.

Since then both Eric Jackson's sons have played decisive parts in the politics of their industry, which like any other needs a pressure group to make its voice heard in the national arena. David followed his father's lead in 1977 while brother Barry became President of the Builders Merchants Federation a few years later in 1981.

Another branch was opened at Sutton-in-Ashfield in 1978 during which year Lincoln and other branches benefited from £2,000,000 worth of improvements. By 1979

turnover reached over £16,500,000 of which profit was somewhat in excess of £1,000,000 this indicates the high proportion taken by overheads such as staff and buildings, not to mention the cost of the very extensive stock which the company offers to its trade and domestic customers. Turnover continued to rise as the family firm spread its wings to provide equipment hire under the name 'Jakhire' and in 1988 bought Corbie Building Supplies of Corby, the former steel town in Northamptonshire.

With a staff of 485 in the late eighties and turnover of £48,000,000 Jackson Shipley had entered the league as one of the top ten among the twenty largest builders merchants in the country. Like other family businesses which believe in the personal touch the Jacksons maintain firm control of the empire created by their own gumption, hard work and intelligence. Their policy for success recognises the importance of a loyal, well trained, long serving staff who not only know their multi-faceted stock but who can relate to the needs of their trade and private customers.

In 1996 the Company celebrated its 50th Anniversary with a change of name to Jackson Building Centres, and in the same year, in line with the customer loyalty cards popular amongst the supermarket chains, the Jacksons have developed their own Jakpoints Cash Card. This computerised 'plastic friend' provides the greatest return for free spending DIY enthusiasts while the Big Spenders amongst trade customers can win every time. These points can be used for entry into sporting events, such as Royal Ascot, and outdoor pursuits from the scenic serenity of hot air ballooning to the most gung-ho of white water rafting.

Top left: A recent picture of Company Chairman, Barry Jackson. Below: An aerial view of the Jackson Building Centre premises on Canwick Road.

Celebrating a century of successful stockbroking

The name of stockbroking firm Hill Osborne & Co will be familiar not only to those with a particular interest in the world of finance, but also to readers of the Lincolnshire Echo following the firm's recent well-publicised triumph in being voted the best medium sized stockbroker in Britain by the readers of the Investors' Chronicle. Hill Osborne & Co has offices in Lincoln, Scarborough, Bradford, Norwich, and in Leicester where the large cut glass engraved vase which was presented to senior partner John Strange in recognition of their success in the Investor's Chronicle reader survey is on display.

This honour, conferred upon the firm as 1998 drew to a close, provided a timely and fitting tribute to a century of service to its clients, as 1999 is the year in which Hill Osborne & Co celebrates its 100th anniversary. To mark the occasion, it seems appropriate to look back at the history of this Lincoln-born firm and the man who founded it.

The firm's very first transaction was effected in October 1899; it is typical of the meticulous efficiency of this firm that it still has the original leather bound ledgers, which show the receipt of £1 10s 5d in respect of new insurance premiums on 26 October 1899. The company, known at that time as J W Hill, was primarily involved in insurance, and was listed in an advertisement in the Lincolnshire Chronicle of that year as an agent of the Sun Insurance Company. J W Hill's first offices were in St Benedict's Square, Lincoln. Its founder, John William Hill, was born on 6 August 1866, the son of a grocer, baker and wholesale confectioner in Kirton-in-Lindsey. John was a Methodist, and was a man of principles; local records show that he signed a Temperance Pledge at Kirton-in-Lindsey on 8 June 1892. On his father's death John became responsible for running the family business and looking after his mother and family. John's chief interest, however, lay in finance, and having fulfilled his responsibilities with regard to his father's business he and his mother moved to Lincoln, where, at the age of 33, he set up in business.

By 1907 J W Hill's offices had moved to City Chambers, 182 High Street, Lincoln. City Chambers were situated on the junction of Lincoln High Street and what is now Wigford Way, above an archway which gave access to a cobbled lane lined with warehouses leading from the High Street to the Brayford Pool. These premises

Top left: J W Hill, *founder of the Company.* **Above:** *The very first documented transaction that the Company carried out.*

overlooked the level crossing, notorious for causing delays to pedestrians and traffic, and the view from the windows was sometimes obscured by the steam and soot which drifted past. The telephone number here was Lincoln 17, and the telegraphic address was Hill Sharebroker, Lincoln. It was during the early 1900s that the emphasis of the business shifted from insurance to stock and share broking; by 1910 J W Hill was being listed in the Lincoln Directory under Stock and Share Brokers.

John, living with his mother at York Place, 9 Sibthorp Street, was a Methodist lay preacher at the Hannah Memorial Chapel, and it was here that he married Mabel Chatterton, of Newland, in May 1910. Mabel's parents were pork pie makers and pastry cooks, with branches of Chatterton & Sons at 36-37 Sincil Street and 90 Newland. John's brother Arthur George Hill, who was five years his junior, was best man, and amongst other gifts the couple were presented with a dozen silver spoons in a case by John's class at the Chapel. They spent their honeymoon in Edinburgh. Their early married life was spent at 8 Rosebery Avenue, and by 1932 they had moved to 49 Beaumont Fee, which was to be John's residence for the rest of his life. John and Mabel had three daughters, Mary, Elizabeth and Ruth, and in due course they were blessed with nine grand-children, of whom one is still with the family firm today. Mary married the Rev Cyril Dorsett and had three children, Ian, Helen and Peter whilst Ruth, having worked for her father between 1936 and 1938, married Ernest A Green and had six children, Andrew, David, Jane, Elizabeth, Stephen, and Peter John who is currently based at the Leicester office and has

worked for the firm for 30 years. Elizabeth, known as Betty, did not marry but assisted her father in the office from 1931 until his death on 23 October 1945.

> "IT IS TYPICAL OF THE METICULOUS EFFICIENCY OF THIS FIRM THAT IT STILL HAS THE ORIGINAL LEDGERS"

Several weeks prior to John Hill's death, he had sold the goodwill of the business to Mr Ralph Strange for the sum of £2,700 under a Partnership Agreement which was to have taken effect on 1 January 1946. John Hill's sudden death on 23 October 1945 brought forward these plans and Mr Strange invited Betty Hill to join him as a Partner. The company changed its name to J W Hill & Co, and Mr Strange took over the role of advising clients while Betty took charge of all the administration. This, of course, was in the days before computers, and all records and ledgers were written up manually. In 1946, after their first year of trading as a partnership, the total revenue was £4,549 and the total profit was £3,577 - an increase of around tenfold over the figures for 1912, when the firm's trading figures had shown a revenue of £449 and a profit of £387. Before very long the workload became too much for two people and they employed a 16-year old school leaver to help them; this was Margaret Jackson, who stayed with the company until her retirement in 1998. Betty Hill herself retired in 1980, having worked for the company for 49 years, 35 of them as a Partner.

Expansion began in a small way in 1956, when J W Hill & Co paid £250 for the goodwill of a stockbroker in Spalding, and Mr Strange ran the business by holding a weekly surgery in a hotel. In 1965 they opened a branch office in Peterborough, and business here

Above: Mr Ralph Strange who bought the goodwill of the business in 1945.

was handled by John Vartan, who in 1967 was admitted as a Partner. In the same year the Lincoln business moved from City Chambers to St Peter's Chambers, 47 Silver Street, following the announcement of plans for the construction of Wigford Way, involving the demolition of the City Chambers offices. In fact these developments were not implemented until many years later.

In 1970 the company's expansion continued with the acquisition of a business in Derby, with R H Blasby becoming a Partner, followed in 1971 by the acquisition of Sir Cyril Osborne's business in Leicester. John Strange, Ralph Strange's eldest son, moved to Leicester to become a Partner of Hill Osborne together with Sir Cyril Osborne's surviving Partner, Walter E Coulson, who remained a Partner until his retirement. The Derby office closed down in 1974 after the retirement of R H Blasby, but the Leicester office has continued to play an important role in the Group's activities.

In 1973 Walter Coulson retired and David Strange, John's brother, was admitted as a Partner.

A major change to trading conditions was introduced in 1974, when provincial Brokers were admitted to trading on the London Stock Exchange directly. Hill Osborne & Co was the first Country firm into London, with George Niblett, formerly of Maguire Roy Marshall, joining the firm as Dealing Partner and opening the London office with Jack Land as Office Manager. The London office continued to operate until 1988, when George Niblett moved to Lincoln and Eric Jones to Leicester.

> "HILL OSBORNE & CO WAS THE FIRST COUNTRY FIRM TO BE ADMITTED TO THE LONDON STOCK EXCHANGE IN 1974"

Below: Lincoln's notorious High Street level crossing, pictured in 1964 where Hill Osborne's offices from the first half of this century can be seen behind the train.

Two new Partners were admitted in 1976: Hugh Stevenson, currently a Partner at the Leicester branch, and Albert Beddie who brought his family business in Grimsby to the Group.

In 1978 Ralph Strange retired and his youngest son, Peter, was admitted as a Partner. Ralph Strange had by then been Senior Partner for 33 years and was largely responsible for building the firm from a very small operation to a thriving regional firm with eight Partners and a network of offices in the East Midlands. He remained with the firm as an active Consultant until his death in 1992.

1978 was also the year in which the introduction of computer technology wrought radical changes to the administration of the Group. Until this time, each office had

Top: Betty Hill, far right, on the occasion of her retirement from the firm in 1980. With her pictured from the left are David Strange, Ralph Strange and Peter Strange.
Right: A member of staff with some of the applications for shares during the privatisation of British Telecom in 1984.

carried out its own administration, but automation through the NMW Computer Bureau, based in Nantwich, made it possible to centralise administration, and Leicester was chosen as the Group's administrative centre. Subsequent major reorganisation of the computer network came in 1990 when the Group set up its own in-house computerised system using Consort Data software. This major investment meant that the company had complete control over its own data, and paved the way for future growth.

By 1984 the company's standing was such that it was asked to act as East Midlands Regional Co-ordinator in the privatisation of British Telecom. This was the first privatisation to be effected, representing the largest ever issue of shares to the public, and Hill Osborne & Co's role was to brief other brokers and intermediaries across the East Midlands. As the issue deadline approached the company's staff rose to the challenge and worked through the night to ensure that all went smoothly, and the ultimate success of the operation resulted in the company being involved in every privatisation that followed.

The Company approaches its centenary with branches at Wigford House, Brayford Wharf East, Lincoln; Permanent House, Horsefair Street, Leicester; 5 Alma Square, Scarborough; Auburn House, 8 Upper Piccadilly, Bradford; and

Jacquard House, Old Bank of England Court, Queen Street, Norwich, the latter having been opened on 1 December 1997. The move from the Royal Insurance Building to Wigford House in Lincoln is also relatively recent, having taken place in January 1998, a year which saw Edward Strange, Chris Hailes and Rupert Fenton admitted as Partners. Edward Strange, the grandson of Ralph Strange and son of John Strange, is a Partner at the Lincoln branch together with John's brothers David and Peter Strange. Chris Hailes joined John Strange, Hugh Stevenson and David Coulson at the Leicester Office, and Rupert Fenton joined Ramsay Fenton at Bradford; this branch had come into the Group in 1985 when Bradford stockbrokers Ramsay Fenton and Albert Henning joined the partnership.

All Hill Osborne & Co's branches provide a personal service to clients, giving advice not only on Stock Exchange business but on other invest-ments and financial planning. Clients include individuals, Trusts, charities and pension funds, and the company encourages close contact with clients, as experience has shown that full discus-sions are of great value in determining upon the

Below: *George Niblett upon his retirement in 1997. Pictured from left to right are: Peter Strange, Hugh Stevenson, John Strange, Ramsay Fenton, George Niblett, David Coulson and David Strange.*

best possible advice. Services include a discretionary management service for those clients who prefer to delegate the management of their investments to the company, which may be combined with a Nominee Service whereby all shareholder communications are sent to Hill Osborne and receive immediate attention; an advisory investment service for clients who wish to make their own investment decisions based on advice tailored to their own individual needs; and dealing services for clients who make their investment decisions independently and require an execution-only dealing facility. Clients who wish to earn a high rate of interest whilst keeping a proportion of their funds readily available can take advantage of the company's deposit facilities with leading financial institutions. The company also advises on personal financial planning matters such as pensions, tax planning, life assurance and school fees; on tax-sheltered investments, personal equity plans and unit trust investments; and it has particular expertise in the field of split capital investment trusts, zero dividend shares and endowment trusts. Its expertise in capital gains tax planning is widely

accepted and further services include the production of a regular newsletter for clients. Most of the firm's research is available on its website - www.hillosborne.co.uk - a medium of communication that John Hill would never have imagined 100 years ago. All advice given by Hill Osborne & Co is totally impartial as the firm is completely independent and free from any ties or potential conflicts of interest.

From the handwritten record of the firm's very first transaction to the most recent computer printout, all Hill Osborne & Co's activities have represented the very best in financial advice to its clients. The success story of this Group is reassuring proof that efficiency, commitment and expertise are qualities which have earned the respect and loyalty of their clients over the last century, and will continue to be appreciated by them in years to come.

Above: John Strange receiving the 'Best Medium Stockbroker of the Year' award from industrialist Sir John Harvey Jones at a glittering reception in London.

'She came, she saw, she was impressed!'

So read the commentary in Turbo News, the company's newspaper, reporting on Mrs Thatcher's visit as Prime Minister to Ruston Gas Turbines in 1982. The Iron Lady, who was not easily impressed, wrote to her hosts, 'You still maintain the best traditions of British engineering and should be very proud of yourselves.'

The company can indeed be proud of its contribution to turbine engineering, having pioneered many improvements and advances over the years. In the field of industrial gas turbines, few companies have equalled the world-wide reputation of ALSTOM Gas Turbines. Their market-leading position has been achieved through the skill and dedication of a workforce whose pride in working for the Company has stood the test of time - a test of more than half a century!

ALSTOM's activities in gas turbines began just after the end of the second world war. The Company was at that time called Ruston and Hornsby, and it was in 1946, following Frank Whittle's pioneering work on jet engines, that Ruston and Hornsby set up a small team known as the Internal Combustion Development Group to investigate the feasibility of designing and producing a long-life industrial gas turbine. In fact, Bob Fielding, a former member of Frank Whittle's Power Jets Company, joined this team.

Initial trials of a prototype, the 3CT, began in 1949, and culminated in a demonstration to engineering correspondents of the British and overseas press. Encouraged by the 3CT's extremely favourable reception, the Company continued development until 1952, when full-scale production of the TA began.

The first order for a TA was placed by the Kuwait Oil Company, and this particular engine, used for gathering centre pumping, has subsequently recorded well in excess of 180,000 operating hours. As news of the reliability and power of the TA spread across the world, other pioneering oil companies were quick to place orders for their production fields, with Iraq Petroleum and AGIP of Italy being amongst the first. Export to the USA began in 1957, when a TA was shipped out and installed in Tulsa; this unit, too, is still operating successfully today for the Williams Brothers Pipeline.

Following the instantaneous success of the TA, the decision was taken to begin work on the development of a 500hp turbine. Designated the TE, it aroused much interest, and the British Admiralty indicated that they would be interested in a more advanced version of the TE for use in their guided

Top left: Sir Frank Whittle the jet pioneer, from whose engine Ruston's first industrial gas turbine, the 3CT, was derived. ***Bottom left:*** *Initial trials of the 3CT began in 1946 culminating in a demonstration to engineers of the British and overseas press.*

Below: *The TA was the first gas turbine to enter full scale production in 1952 and the first order was received from the Kuwait Oil Company for gathering centre pumping.*

put into production in a range of sizes. The first technology demonstration model, the TG, developed a staggering output of 8,350hp. The smaller-scale production model which followed, the TD4000, developed 4,000hp and design work began in 1967; tests on the first unit were completed in 1969.

At this stage it was felt that the volume of turbine production by Ruston and Hornsby was sufficient to justify a company in its own right, and Ruston Gas Turbines was formed.

On-going development work on the TA range resulted in the introduction of the 1620hp TA1500 in 1964, followed by the 1833hp TA1750 in 1970. Further improvement and development culminated in an engine producing 2500hp.

missile ships; and so the 1300hp TF was developed, with a number of them being installed in Navy ships in 1961.

The recovery of exhaust heat to improve the overall efficiency was recognised in the early stages of turbine development as an important factor in the economics of gas turbines, and Ruston was selling and installing gas turbines with waste heat recovery long before the concept 'Total Energy' was invented.

One of the first of these total energy installations was built into the Park Plaza Shopping Centre at Little Rock, the state capital of Arkansas, where for several years it provided all the light, heat and refrigeration requirements for the entire complex.

Ruston continued to develop and market the TA, TE and TF turbines, and in 1964 the decision was made to move into the larger engine range. The plan was to perfect an aerodynamic and thermal design which would then be

Meanwhile, the success of the new TD4000 continued. The Greater London Council placed an

Top left: The TA assembly line as it looked in 1969. Right: In 1964, Ruston made the decision to enter the larger engine range. The TD4000 was the first of these larger engines to enter full scale production and had a rating of 4,000hp. Design work began in 1967 and the first unit completed tests in 1969.

Left: Installing a TA compressor into the stator assembly in 1970. Bottom: Another Ruston gas turbine leaves the factory in the 1970s.

packaged sets allowing the pre-testing of the engine to reduce installation and on-site costs. Orders for the TB3000 followed swiftly, with eight pump sets being purchased in 1971 by an Argentine oil company for a crude oil pipe line.

A continuing programme of development ensued, with the Company's work geared towards anticipating new market requirements as well as satisfying existing markets. By 1971 Ruston

order for two generating sets for its Northern Outfall Sewage Works at Beckton, where it already had eight Ruston TA gas turbines which had been installed in 1958. As the TD4000 became more and more successful it became evident that there was a market in oil and gas industries for 3,000bhp turbines that could drive pumps and compressors. A compact unit was needed for this application, so it would be necessary to reduce the length without compromising the accessibility which had become a characteristic of Ruston engines. The design produced was similar to that of the TD4000, and the new unit was designated the TB3000. With its launch, the company also introduced the concept of

had nearly 500 units in operation, and between them they had accumulated over 12,000,000 running hours. By constantly evaluating and monitoring these engines, Ruston was able to assess how engines could be refined and the power output of each unit safely increased. The output of the TB3000 was increased to 3,920hp, then to 4,900hp; then, by using technology developed on other turbines, to 5,200hp, with a subsequent increase to 5,400hp for use with gas fuel only.

Orders were by now coming in from all over the world. The name of Ruston had become synonymous with quality, integrity and power, and

the Company was becoming a leading force in the design, development and installation of gas turbines. Over 90 per cent of Lincoln's production was exported, and of this nearly 80 per cent was destined for the oil industry; Ruston gas turbines were used by every major oil company. Their uses included electricity generation, oil pumping and compressor drive, both onshore and offshore, in a variety of extreme climatic conditions from Arctic wastes to Equatorial deserts.

A total of 41 offshore platform sets was installed on the immense Shell flood water recovery scheme in Lake Maracaibo, Venezuela, and also in Cook Inlet, Alaska, providing power to the Atlantic Richfield Company's drilling platform. TD4000s and TB3000s were used on BP's first super platforms in the North Sea Forties Field, and TA1750 generating sets were installed on Shell's Auk Field platform. Orders for onshore units came from Iran, Algeria and Kuwait as well as Argentina and Qatar.

Demand for total energy units also increased; 12 TAs were installed at the John Player tobacco factory in Nottingham, and

Top left: Celebration of the 1000th Ruston gas turbine during the Open Day in 1977. Distinguished guests included Sir Henry Neville (Lord Lieutenant of Lincolnshire) and his wife, the Mayor of Lincoln and the Sheriff of Lincoln with their ladies. Also pictured is Margaret Jackson. Right: One of eight TB3000 pump sets destined for Yacimientos Petroliferos Fiscales (Argentina) in 1971 for use on the Challacao to Puerto Rosales pipeline.

four TD4000 generating sets with exhaust heat boilers were installed at the Singer Company in Clydebank to create the largest gas turbine total energy plant in Europe at that time. This installation also set another record, with progression from receipt of order to full working capacity taking only 18 months.

The Tornado, introduced in 1981, began a trend towards using the names of storms for products. Developing 8,500hp, it combined new technology, advances in metallurgy and new design methods while still retaining the renowned Ruston reputation for reliability, endurance and minimal maintenance. The Tornado was a compact unit for use in packaged sets and, as with the earlier TB3000, careful attention was given to ancillary equipment, its modular design and location, in order to simplify and expedite servicing and maintenance. Ruston also took this opportunity to introduce an advanced control system employing digital technology, to meet the market requirement for more sophisticated controls.

Ruston began packaging large engines at Lincoln in 1984, initially with 15 and 25MW units that used Rolls Royce gas generators and later with the RLM range which used gas generators built by GE of America. This initial venture led to collaboration between GE and Ruston on a number of projects involving aero-derivative engines and component parts for aero engines, which still continues today.

In 1987 it was announced that development work had begun on two new engines, the Hurricane, rated at 1.5MW, and the Typhoon, rated at 4MW. Designed for electrical power generation, the Typhoon was eminently suitable for combined heat

Left: In 1982 Margaret Thatcher became the first British Prime Minister to visit Ruston Gas Turbines. It was Ruston's impressive record of sales and growth that had prompted the visit.

quality, reliability and endurance remained the same.

Meanwhile, following the Typhoon's success at its first introductory rating, in 1992 its power was increased to 4.55MW. A further version of the Typhoon, introduced in 1994, was designed specifically for driving pumps and compressors for the oil and gas industries. With a power output of 6,400hp it incorporated a high level of gas turbine and package commonality with its single shafted brother. Subsequent technological improvements enabled the output of the Typhoon to be increased to 4.91MW on natural gas fuel.

Development of the Tornado continued and a more powerful version, delivering 8,900hp, was introduced. To date over 200 Tornado units have been sold, and their combined operating time already exceeds 8 million hours.

The next introduction to the EGT range was the Tempest. Launched in 1995, this unit was designed

and power (CHP) applications; it was launched onto the world market in 1989 and again orders were secured, the first for three units in the UK and Spain.

Continued development of the microprocessor-based control system, which was now available for all engines in the Ruston range, led to the Rustronic MkII system offering increased performance, quicker response time, increased reliability and greater compactness.

Ruston Gas Turbines had become a GEC subsidiary in the late 1960s. In 1989 the turbine interests of GEC and Alcatel Alsthom were merged by the creation of GEC ALSTHOM, and shortly afterwards European Gas Turbines (EGT) was formed, with GE of America taking a minority shareholding. The name was new, but the commitment to

Below: One of two British Petroleum platforms in the Forties Field. Each platform is equipped with 8 Ruston gas turbines totalling 35,000hp, driving generators for production drilling, main line oil pumps and the platform's gas compressors. Right: Two 4.56MW Typhoon gas turbines installed at Tioxide Europe Ltd., Grimsby. Power generated is absorbed by site services and exhaust heat is used to dry gypsum for the manufacture of plaster board.

for electrical power generation with an output of 7.5MW and, as with all EGT products, was based on proven technology; the Tempest is, in essence, a scaled version of the Typhoon which achieves higher output and complements the other gas turbines in the EGT portfolio.

The Cyclone, the latest product to be launched, has an output of over 13MW. Incorporating the proven technology of the Tempest, the Cyclone offers cost-effective power for a multitude of duties including offshore platforms, industrial power generation and pipeline transmission.

The Cyclone complements the existing family of industrial machines from ALSTOM - the Typhoon, Tornado and Tempest - incorporating the latest in aerodynamic design and emissions technology. It is an extension of the Tempest gas turbine with the addition of a zero stage to the air compressor, a two-stage compressor turbine and a two-stage free

power turbine which take advantage of the increased mass flow and higher pressure ratio to produce a higher simple cycle efficiency.

As with all the gas turbines designed and developed by the Company over more than 50 years, it embodies the skills and expertise of a workforce committed to excellence in engineering.

From the TA to the Cyclone, the Company owes a debt of gratitude to those who have striven over the years to uphold its traditions, designing and producing world-beating gas turbines, over 3,000 of which are in service in 81 countries, and have between them accumulated over 170 million running hours.

Following the flotation of GEC Alsthom in 1998, a new company called ALSTOM was formed and European Gas Turbines changed its name to ALSTOM Gas Turbines.

ALSTOM is now Lincoln's largest industrial employer, with around 2800 staff and a turnover exceeding £300 million. Seventy-five per cent of sales are exported and the Company boasts seven Queen's Awards, five for export, one for technology and one for environmental work.

Above: Assembling the turbine stator of a Tempest gas turbine in 1996. Below: ALSTOM today, a high technology, world leading company in the heart of historic Lincoln.

The factory that has gone from steam loco to semi-conductors in 80 years

The Lincoln Civic Award is made annually "to express the thanks of the citizens of Lincoln to an organisation for an achievement which has brought credit to the City, and itself is of outstanding merit", and in 1981 this Award was won by English Electric Valve in Carholme Road. EEV was responsible for the development of a magnetron which is now used in virtually 100 per cent of linear accelerators used in hospitals for the treatment of cancer. A magnetron is a valve which controls magnetic impulses, and its development came about as a result of EEV's programme of research in the field of electronics, which has also led to pioneering work in the area of semiconductors, transistors and integrated circuits.

The Carholme Road factory's involvement in the manufacture of technologically-advanced products began in 1956; before then, the site had been home to a very different kind of activity. The factory was built just after the war for a firm of joinery manufacturers, H Newsum and Sons. Their products included everything from kitchen cupboards destined for local households to pre-fabricated wooden houses destined for erection anywhere from London to Australia. Timber was brought up the Fossdyke Canal by barge to the back of the works, where in the very early days it was unloaded by crane and

carried manually to the store where it was stacked manually. Later, a small steam locomotive was used; the train crossed the canal by means of a swing bridge - its foundations can still just be seen behind the factory - and delivered the timber directly into the

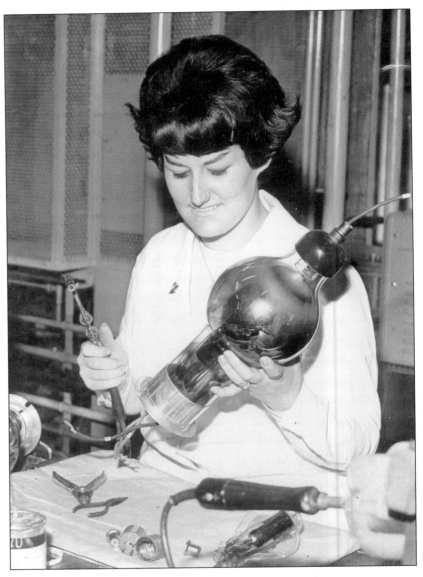

works. H Newsum and Sons' family business survived the second world war and began to prosper in the period immediately afterwards when the demand for new homes was high, but it then ran into serious financial difficulties, and as a result the Newsum family had to close the Lincoln works in the mid-50s.

Meanwhile, the British Thompson Houston Company, based in Rugby, was experiencing serious difficulty in attracting female labour to its factory in Lutterworth, near Leicester, and finally they decided that the only solution was to move; Plymouth and Lincoln were identified as possible locations, and they opted for Lincoln because it was closer to the

Top right: *Assembly of rectifier.*
Left: *Glass-Metal sealing.*

Left: Sputter-Etching of thin film.
Below: An aerial view of the premises.

while the third had been turned into a training centre. The investment paid off, however, because there were no staffing problems in Lincoln; applicants, both male and female were queuing up for jobs.

By 1960 the factory had over 750 employees. That year developments made at the company's Rugby Research Laboratory put the company into a position where it was able to begin manufacturing thyristors, and Lincoln became the first factory in Britain to begin thyristor production. Three years later Lincoln became the first manufacturer in Britain to put a fully diffused thyristor into production.

head office in Rugby. They acquired Newsum's old factory in Carholme Road, which needed an immense amount of work. There was a great deal of debris to to be cleared away, and several outbuildings had to be demolished. New flooring, suspended ceilings and brick walls for the sides and ends of most of the bays had to be installed, and complete electrical rewiring and redecoration was needed. A new office block was built at the front of the factory and the canteen was refurbished and extended. Meanwhile, limited production had begun in two of the existing pre-fabricated bungalows,

In November 1964 the valve side of the business, which had been in Lincoln since 1958, was bought by English Electric Limited. This acquisition enabled EEV to add to its product range. The factory building was divided into two, with AEI Electronics concentrating on semiconductors in one half, while at the South West end of the factory English Electric Valve was producing magnetrons and spark gaps and later TR tubes and semiconductors. EEV was

the first company in the world to produce a combination of TR tubes and semiconductors, which greatly improved protection for radar receivers, and Lincoln continued to develop these products for applications in both military and commercial radars. Two new production lines were set up to meet the requirements for trigatrons and monitor diodes, previously supplied by Elliott Automation which had been taken over by EEV. At the same time the production of welder ignitrons was greatly expanded, to the point where they were supplied to every car manufacturer in the UK and widely exported.

During 1966 two serious fires occurred at the factory. The first happened in May, when an oxy-acetylene torch set the roof alight, and the resulting blaze destroyed a bay in English Electric Valve's half of the factory. Then the day before the beginning of the Christmas holiday another fire broke out, started this time by a carelessly-discarded cigarette in AEI's stores, and a considerable number of finished devices was destroyed.

In June 1967, AEI became AEI-Thorn Semiconductors Ltd, and Thorn transferred their transistor manufacture from their site at Brimsdown to Lincoln. This was to be a short-lived association, however, because five months later, the General Electric Company Limited (GEC) made a successful bid for AEI, and on February 1st 1968 the company became AEI Semiconductors Ltd.

The Lincoln factory underwent a number of changes in 1968. AEI Semiconductors began manufacturing integrated circuits, and was at that time the only facility within GEC to do so. However, in September of that year GEC and English Electric merged, and as English Electric already had two large integrated circuit operations, one at Witham in Essex and one at Glenrothes in Scotland, development of integrated circuits at Lincoln ceased at the end of the year.

GEC's three manufacturing sites, at Witham, Glenrothes and Lincoln, were brought under one umbrella in 1969 with the formation of GEC Semiconductors Limited. The factory at Glenrothes was later closed, as was the Witham factory some

*Above: Gold wire bonding. **Below:** The Magnetron Team with their Lincoln Civic Award.*

time afterwards, but the MOS work was transferred from Witham to a GEC Semiconductor facility at the Hirst Research Laboratory, and this re-grew, forming the basis of what eventually became the Integrated Circuit Division at Doddington Road, Lincoln.

In 1970, at the beginning of what was to be a decade of rapid growth, the Active Module Group was transferred to Kidsgrove. There was a severe shortage of space at the Lincoln factory; the Stores and part of Inspection had been moved out to a building on the Sunningdale Trading Estate in the Spring of 1969, where they remained for two years, but as turnover continued to increase more shop-floor space was required. Work began on a new three-storey factory at Carholme Road, and when it was completed in 1975 it provided almost double the manufacturing area. In 1979 work started on three bays at at the Doddington Road site, and the following Spring the Power Hybrid and Microwave divisions were moved from Carholme Road to Doddington Road. A further two bays were completed in 1981 to accommodate IC manufacture; with the formation of a new company within the Marconi Group called Marconi Electronic Devices Limited, Lincoln had become integrated into the activities of the Integrated Circuit Group at Wembley and the Hybrid Group at Portsmouth, and production was gradually transferred from Wembley to Doddington Road during the course of 1981. A new office block was built and the Doddington Road factory was officially opened in September 1981.

Marconi Electronic Devices Limited became part of GEC-Plessey Semiconductors, and, in 1996, was bought by EEV. In acquiring GPS, EEV acquired key technology to add to its existing base, putting

it in a powerful and unique position as a leader in the merging markets for microwave application. These markets include communications and automotive applications as well as the core military and commercial markets. EEV moved the business back onto the Carholme Road site, giving the history of the company a pleasing symmetry; the manufacture of Magnetrons and Spark Gaps, products made by 'traditional' processes, was transferred to the company headquarters at Chelmsford, Essex, in 1999.

Eighty years of manufacturing activity at Carholme Road have changed the site almost beyond recognition, both in terms of factory buildings and output. EEV won the Queens Award for Technological Innovation in 1983, and is at the cutting edge of technology. The joinery workshop with its woodshavings and sawdust has made way for ultra-clean rooms and precision equipment, and the hi-tech components made here today would have been quite inconceivable to the workforce of H Newsun and Sons, for whom technology was a steam train to transport wood from one end of the site to the other.

Top left: Just a few of the products produced at EEV. Left: A Tornado encompassing critical EEV radar components. Below: A Rapier Missile using several key EEV components.

Building on Lincoln's tradition of artistic and land-based skills

Lincoln, with its castle, its Roman archway and its many fine buildings, is a truly historic city with a fine architectural heritage and a long tradition of craftsmanship and fine art. It has been a trading centre since Viking times, a cathedral city since 1072, and home to one of the country's greatest Schools of Art since 1863.

It is also a university city, with the students of De Montfort University playing an important part in city life. De Montfort University's presence in Lincoln came with its amalgamation, in 1994, with two of Lincoln's long-established and highly respected institutions, the Lincolnshire School of Art and Design and the Lincolnshire College of Agriculture and Horticulture.

The Great Exhibition of 1951 created a new awareness of the need for 'systematic training for designers in the field of applied and industrial design'. In Lincoln, a committee was set up to oversee the establishment of a School of Art, with the Rev J S Gibney as its secretary. The opening of Lincoln School of Art and Design in the Corn Exchange on Monday 2 February, 1863 can be attributed largely to his energy and commitment. The following year the school moved to Silver Street, where it was to remain for 22 years before becoming half of the School of Science and Art on Monks Road in 1885. From the outset students of School were keen to make their mark, and their activities included exhibiting each year in Kensington, London. The School's reputation grew, and official recognition came in 1924 when the School was confirmed as one of the country's established Schools for Art and Design.

In 1957 the School was re-established independently at Christ's Hospital Terrace, next to the Church of

St Michael on the Mount. This was formerly the church of Rev Gibney, who did so much for the School before being killed in a tragic accident in 1871, when, in the course of inspecting the art school roof, he slipped and fell through a skylight.

Full diplomas in design were introduced in 1948, and by 1952 students' success in gaining entry to the Royal College of Art had further enhanced the School's

reputation. By 1961 the School was one of the country's major design providers, offering courses in Graphics, Textiles, Fashion, 3D and Photography as well as Fine Art and Printing.

The School moved to its site at the Greestone Building in 1975. Designed in 1893 by the architect William Watkins, this attractive

*Top right: Art students in the composition and painting room in 1960. **Above:** An evening gown designed and made in the Dress Department in 1959. **Left:** Agricultural students learning the skill of ploughing during the 1950s.*

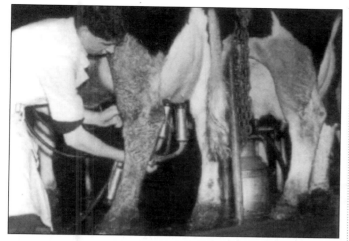

building, with its elaborately decorated exterior, has been sympathetically renovated inside to provide extensive studio, library, exhibition and lecture facilities.

The institution - re-named Lincolnshire College of Art and Design in 1985 - expanded into Silvergate House and Free School Lane in 1993 to provide more space for the BA programmes in Fashion and Graphic Design. The following year Lincolnshire College of Art and Design amalgamated with De Montfort University, which also has centres in Leicester, Bedford and Milton Keynes, to become DMU Lincoln School of Art and Design.

Following amalgamation further degree programmes were introduced along with Masters degrees in Conservation Science, Fine Art and Dyslexia Studies. In 1995 De Montfort University's School of Art and Design moved its administrative headquarters to Chad Varah House, formerly the city's Theological College.

This amalgamation also incorporated the Lincolnshire College of Agriculture and Horticulture, founded at the end of the second world war to remedy the severe shortage of people with the skills needed to get the farming sector back on its feet. Kesteven Farm Institute began training ex-servicemen at Caythorpe Court in 1948, and Lindsey Farm Institute began courses at Riseholme the following year. Over the years course content has constantly evolved to meet the changing needs of the farming communities whose needs they serve, with increased mechanisation in the 60s and the introduction of the Common Agricultural Policy in the 70s calling for

the acquisition of new skills. In 1980 the countrywide decline in the rural economy resulted in Kesteven Farm Institute, now called Kesteven Agricultural College, and Lindsey Farm Institute, now called Lindsey College of Agriculture, joining with Holbeach Agricultural Centre to form the Lincolnshire College of Agriculture and Horticulture.

DMU Lincoln has, since amalgamation, developed a strong academic provision including an extensive, and growing, range of degree courses in the established specialist areas, and offers excellent facilities for land-based studies on one of the most profitable university farms in the country. Excellent facilities are provided on campus, and, in support of its commitment to increased access, progression and guidance at all levels from Further Education to postgraduate study and research. Above all, De Montfort University is firmly committed to building on the centre's history of educational provision and achieving excellence in the specialist areas of Arts and Design and Agriculture and Horticulture, and to actively contributing to community and cultural initiatives in the city and throughout Lincolnshire.

Top left: Just one aspect of agricultural husbandry taught at the university. **Left:** *The cover of the School of Art prospectus for the academic year 1960-61.*
Below: *Greestone building, home to DMU Lincoln's Fine Art Department.*

LINCOLN SCHOOL OF ART PROSPECTUS

60
61

Generations of learning at North Lincolnshire College

Today North Lincolnshire College is the largest educational institution in the County, with around 9,000 students of whom 2,500 are full-time. The College has an extensive curriculum which embraces degree, technician and craft level courses, basic skill courses, GCSE, "A" Level and Access programmes.

The College developed from the Science faculty of the School of Science and Art, which opened on 27th September 1886, on a site at the beginning of Monks Road donated by Lincoln Corporation.

In 1893 purpose-built engineering workshops were added on the north side of the original building at a cost of £1,478 2s 3d. Then, in 1901, the school was handed over to the Corporation and renamed The City of Lincoln Municipal Technical School.

A significant development took place in 1923 with the introduction of National Certificates in Mechanical Engineering for apprentices employed in the city's engineering industries. The then headmaster, Mr. Collis, ensured that the school was one of the first in the country to adopt this scheme characterising the traditional close working relationship between the school and Lincoln's major industries.

Then, in 1928, the school became the Lincoln Technical College adopting its own premises on Cathedral Street in July 1932. An extension was added to this building in August 1937.

During 1947 the Education Committee came to the conclusion that the Junior Technical courses held at the College should be terminated and the future need for these courses should be met by the Grammar and Modern schools under the new system of education.

Costing approximately £60,000, the new extension for the Building Department was officially opened in October 1957 and was situated adjacent to the existing Cathedral buildings, contrasting significantly with the architecture of the 1930s.

A large new extension was added in 1961 to coincide with Commonwealth Training Week. Situated on a sloping site on the west side of Abbey Street, it contained five floors and cost £5,194,489.00. This extension was part of a long term plan for a large Technical College in Lincoln and plans had been laid down to occupy the building used by the City School.

Top right: *The college pictured in 1957.*
Left: *Engineering workshops pictured in 1932.*

1964 saw the purchase of the NAAFI Club on Park Street which was renamed the Further Education Centre.

Work began on a further extension on the site of the old Lincoln Corporation abattoir in 1967 to provide first-class up-to-date accommodation for the College, replacing buildings on Temple Street as well as the old Ragged School on Sparrow Lane.

In 1978 a further extension to the College was added. It was built on the lower half of the site previously occupied by the City Abattoir and Cattle Market and incorporated administration, business and management studies, mechanical engineering, electrical engineering and communal facilities including the sports hall. The larger areas - the motor vehicle workshops and the sports hall - became a multi-storey unit in the centre of the site. The rest of the accommodation was divided into smaller blocks.

In September 1987 North Lincolnshire College was formed from the merger of Lincoln College of Technology and Gainsborough College of Further Education and in April 1993 separated from the County Council becoming an independent incorporate Organisation with charitable status.

In order to provide for more students a new Flexible Learning Centre was opened in 1993 on the third floor of the Abbey Building and the Refectory was re-furbished and renamed the Abbey Diner. At the same time a new reception area was completed on Monks Road bringing together Guidance Services and the General Office.

The Halls of Residence, comprising 115 study bedrooms were started in January 1994 and a new

site on Acland Street in Gainsborough, focusing on further and adult education, commenced construction, finishing in July 1995.

Latest developments include the complete renovation of Sessions House, a redundant Georgian listed building which once housed the Magistrates' Court, Police Station, Fire Station and a number of cells. This has been carefully restored in order to retain important historical detail while also offering state-of-the-art training facilities to students. In the old building catering students serve the public in the restaurant and bar, with childcare facilities and music practice rooms accommodated in the refurbished cells. A brand new purpose-built Student Union block stands alongside complementing the architecture of the past.

The College, in recognition of the training needs of adults in the latest Information Technology, has also opened a 'shop' on the High Street where a drop-in service is offered.

North Lincolnshire College has seen many changes in demography, in educational demand and in the type of people who seek learning. It is hoped that, by responding to the needs of the whole community, the College will still be training the people of Lincolnshire and beyond well into the next millennium.

Top left and above: The newly refurbished entrance to the college and the spacious reception.
Below: Sessions House, recently renovated to offer state-of-the-art training facilities to students.

Where exemplary healthcare is complemented by the best standards of comfort

Patients at the Bromhead Hospital today are impressed above all by the comprehensive range of modern medical and surgical equipment and the high standards of comfort in the carefully furnished ensuite rooms; and they may find it hard to believe, as they make their selection from the full a la carte and special menus available, that care for the sick began on this site in a very rudimentary way as long ago as 1865.

The Bromhead Institution was founded by Mrs Anne Fector Bromhead, who, with her own health failing at the age of almost 60, decided to do what she could to remedy the extreme inadequacy of the equipment and the nursing at the Lincoln County Hospital. The 80 beds and six day nurses could barely cope with the regular outbreaks of fever in the town; there was only one bath in the hospital, and the only source of hot water was a little boiler up two flights of stairs. Mrs Bromhead and some friends began raising funds; by 1867 it had been possible to provide a new ward and other improvements, and an Institution for Nurses had been set up, employing in that year 15 nurses, 10 of whom had been trained in the best London hospitals. The nurses attended those needing care in their own homes for a fee of one guinea a week, but this fee was reduced or waived altogether in the case of the sick or poor. There are on record many reports of appreciation of the nurses' goodness and devotion; after one epidemic of infectious fever in Scothern all the inhabitants of the village joined together to make them a presentation.

The institution continued to grow, with the work being carried on after Mrs Bromhead's death in 1886 by her daughter Miss Henrietta Bromhead. The Bromhead Nursing Home was built as a memorial to Mrs Bromhead, and has subsequently been extended at various times. A nearby house presented in 1907 as a memorial to Miss Bromhead was used as nurses' home and administration block, and is now St Barnabas Hospice. An adjoining property was acquired in 1930 and served as a private maternity home until Maternity was moved into the main building in 1937; the building then became the sleeping quarters for the nurses and was renamed Dormer House.

Top right: The Bromhead Nursing Home and Maternity Wing in the early 1900s. *Top left:* Ann Fector Bromhead, founder of the Hospital. *Left:* The Operating Theatre and Anaesthetic room in the Nursing Home. *Below:* A very stark labour room in the early 1900s.

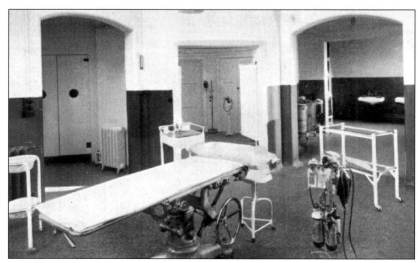

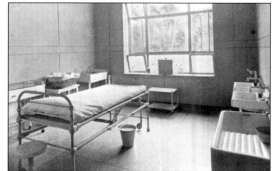

Health Screening, Well Woman and Breast Screening.

The Bromhead's staff of around 45 nurses is trained to the very highest standards; the hospital has a firm commitment to training, also providing external training to nursing homes and care institutions and running a range of courses in collaboration with De Montfort University.

In 1998 the hospital achieved ISO 9002 accreditation. This means that the hospital works to consistent quality standards audited externally by the British Standards Institute.

In 1948 the hospital was taken over by the NHS, and remained part of the NHS until 1981, when following a Lincolnshire-wide appeal the hospital was bought back. Since then it has operated as an independent hospital with the status of non-profit making charitable trust, and the reinvestment of all surplus revenue has resulted in Bromhead Hospital becoming one of the most modern and sophisticated health care centres in the region. An extensive range of medical and surgical treatments and services are available, with facilities for emergency admissions, and an after-care service. The high specification facilities incorporate the very latest in theatre technology, a fully equipped radiology department and a complete range of pathological and pharmaceutical facilities. Having kept at the forefront of technological developments, the hospital is equipped to carry out an increasing variety of innovative techniques, with a growing list of surgical procedures performed using Minimal Invasive Surgery. The Bromhead also employs very sophisticated diagnostic techniques, and in the early 1990s was the first hospital in Lincolnshire to introduce Magnetic Resonance Imaging. In 1998 it was also the first hospital in the county to offer a Cardiac Catheterisation service.

The 40 single rooms all have the capability for intensive monitoring, and the hospital's resident doctor provides 24 hour medical cover. Bromhead is recognised by all major insurance companies and is a Preferred Provider for BUPA, and patients without private health insurance pay a guaranteed 'fixed price' for surgery. Thus it is open to all who wish to choose independent healthcare to benefit from the Bromhead's high quality services, complemented by a warm, comfortable, reassuring environment where patients can relax and convalesce safe in the knowledge that their individual needs and expectations will be met in a prompt, caring and ethical manner.

Top left: The imposing facade of the Bromhead Institution pictured around 1905 (now St. Barnabas Hospice). Above: The modern hi-tech facilities of today's hospital. Below: The entrance to the hospital as it appears today.

Modern surgical techniques permit an increasing number of patients to be treated as out-patients, and the hospital's comprehensive out-patient facilities include an endoscopy unit, radiology facilities, and a physiotherapy suite with a well-equipped gymnasium and two separate assessment/treatment rooms. A number of specialist clinics are held in areas where preventative measures are recommended, such as Bone Densitometry, Menopause, Family Planning,

From wartime service to luxury living

The Old Hall was built in 1735 by Lord Vere Bertie in the heart of what was soon to become the famous 'Shires' hunting country. He was son of the first Duke of Ancaster while the Vere name had connections with the Dukes of St Albans, Hereditary Grand Falconers of England, who were descended from an alliance between Nell Gwynne's son and a daughter of the Earl of Oxford.

During the nineteenth century the Branston Hall estate passed to the Honourable Alexander Leslie Melville, a name famous in fox hunting circles. He replaced what became the Old Hall with the Elizabethan style building which is now the hotel. It was fourteen years in building by the London firm of Lawrence and Sons to the design of McVicar and Son. Victorian country house owners, unlike their more careless Georgian ancestors, were adamant that the sexes were kept apart as were family and servants in their separate quarters. It is easy to detect the taller more spacious family apartments from those in the narrow-corridored, lower ceilinged service wing linked to the Kitchen Court, an open yard surrounded by small specialist stores and work rooms.

While daughters of the house and their guests would enjoy comfortable bedrooms in the main block, the sons and single male guests would be accommodated in more Spartan rooms for which their years of incarceration in bleak public schools had prepared them. It was usual for former homes such as the now redundant Old Hall to be designated as the Dower House to which the heir's widowed mother would retire on the accession of her son. In this case it became the home, in 1899, of the estate's steward or farm manager and some of the staff not accommodated in the new hall. The Old Hall was burnt down on New Year's Day 1903.

The inter-war years' history of Branston Hall was fairly typical of smaller country houses of the period when the landed gentry, decimated out of all proportion to its size by the carnage of the Great War, struggled against punitive taxation to keep farming estates in business during an era which declined into the Depression.

Branston Hall, like so many such houses throughout Britain, received its call up papers for National Service during World War Two. The spacious rooms of the Hall were converted to war time use as an RAF hospital providing wards and

Above: Branston Hall Hotel, a magnificent country house hotel set amidst 88 acres of wooded parkland.

building had fallen into disuse and was as sadly neglected as any dowager who had seen better days. Two years later it was sold at auction to a private company which lavishly restored it to its Edwardian glory. Little of the estate remains, as much had been previously sold off. Hotel guests can look out onto some 88 acres of wooded parkland which provide a protective screen and a worthy setting for this lovely house.

Today Branston Hall Country House Hotel thrives in beautiful serene surroundings which enhance the service provided by staff at all levels working to transport guests into an era when wishes were immediately provided. The Hall caters for both the extra special wedding which requires an elegance and splendour beyond the norm and for the small intimate gathering which many prefer.

The needs of the business world for comfortable, well equipped and professionally serviced naturally lit function suites and conference rooms to impress are as much part of the Hall's management expertise as the more traditional duties of the hotelier. The whole package of facilities, which include a Fitness Suite, can be tailored to suit business clients' requests for refreshments, buffet and/or silver service meals with or without overnight accommodation.

All guests are special to the dedicated staff of Branston Hall Hotel.

accommodation for medical staff. The spacious grounds were ideal for quiet convalescence far from the noise and discomfort of aerial combat. The RAF was virtually unique in that its warriors took off from their home ground to fight and then returned when work finished for drinks in village pubs, that is if circumstances of survival and discipline allowed.

After the war the Hall and its estate were taken over by the council who continued to run the hospital. Unfortunately by 1980 the

Top left: The pleasant atmosphere of the Branston Hall Lakeside Restaurant. Above: The Churchill Suite, a popular venue for private functions, parties and weddings. Below: An attractive line drawing of Branston Hall Hotel as seen from the lake.

The family firm that makes its customers feel at home

Homebuyers looking at new developments today expect to be able to inspect a fully fitted and furnished show house, and indeed seeing the completed product, walking around inside, seeing whether one feels at home and whether one can imagine living there, makes the decision as to whether or not to buy much easier. But show homes are in fact a relatively new concept, and one of the first seen in the City of Lincoln was at the Lakeside development in 1956.

The Lakeside development was built by the Lincoln firm of Dixon and Hogg, a firm which is about to celebrate 50 years in business. It was started by a young man named Eric Dixon, a time-served joiner from school who had worked for a local company before setting up as a contract joiner. He was joined by a plumber friend, Dennis Hogg, and the partnership thrived. Having established themselves as contractors and gained experience of the business climate and trends in the local construction industry, they felt confident enough to start their own company to build housing.

In the late 1950s housing was in short supply because of the increase in population. Also, as the economy recovered after the war, more people found themselves in a position where they were able to afford to buy their own homes. There was great demand for well designed, good quality houses which gave value for money, and this was the section of the market which Dixon and Hogg aimed to supply.

The company's first housing development was at Sunningdale Drive, Lincoln, and was completed in 1955. The Lakeside development, featuring their first show house, was built in 1956.

Since those early days the company has been

Top right: Dixon and Hogg's first 'Showhouse' at the Lakeside development in 1956.
Left: The lounge of a 1950s showhome.

customer expectations, but the firm remains keen to maintain its reputation for building well-designed, good quality houses which represent value for money in every price bracket. It is still a family-run organisation; Dennis Hogg sadly died in the 1970s, and the business is now run by a management team composed of John Dixon who has run the company as Managing Director since 1983, and June Gauke, Sales Director since 1986. Eric Dixon has now retired but still remains Chairman of the company. The family values which customers have come to expect are still very much in evidence, and this is something which the whole group is very keen to maintain.

involved in a great many successful housing projects in Lincolnshire. The range of housing for which Dixon and Hogg has been responsible over the years covers a wide variety of styles and prices, from keenly-priced homes for the first-time buyer to individual residences designed and built to the buyer's own specifications.

Dixon and Hogg is today a limited company, trading as DH Homes from the premises in Mint Street, Lincoln, a characterful old building which it has occupied for many years. These premises are in themselves a fine piece of architecture. Formerly a chapel, many of its original features have been preserved.

Expansion and technological progress have inevitably brought many changes in working practices, but essentially the principles on which the firm operates have changed surprisingly little over the years. Now offering a vast selection of styles and specialising in exclusive, individually-designed properties, the specification of all the houses it builds, from the largest to the smallest, are constantly being updated and improved to incorporate the latest developments in domestic fittings and keep ahead of

Top left: A modern 1990s Showhouse. *Below:* A 1990s style lounge. *Bottom:* A kitchen from one of Dixon and Hogg's modern showhomes.

Planning the best route to success

From Model T Fords to air-conditioned tractor units; from milk to dinosaurs; from Lincoln to Lyon; Denby Transport has been there, done that, and become a well-known international haulage company, operating a fleet of some 150 vehicles and carrying for blue-chip customers at home and on the Continent.

The company is now run by Peter Denby. His father Dick is current Chairman, and it was Dick's father Bill who started the business during the general strike of 1926, investing £100 in a second-hand one-ton Model T Ford truck with solid tyres and oil lamps, and taking farmers' milk to the dairies around Lincoln when the strike brought the railways to a halt. The service provided by 19 year old Bill Denby was flexible and above all reliable, and the farmers were happy to leave their custom with him, even though road transport was more expensive than rail. This emphasis on added value service has remained fundamental to the company's policy ever since, and time and again they have won custom by competing not only on price but on delivery performance and safety.

Today, Denby Transport specialises in continental haulage, with France remaining the core market. By the end of the 1970s 100 round trips a month were being made to destinations in all parts of France. In recent years the company has come under pressure to extend its operations, but, by nature cautious and conservative, it has resisted too-rapid expansion. International haulage is a competitive business and one which holds many pitfalls, and a cautious approach is essential for long-term success. For instance, a major consideration when considering expansion is traffic flow, as no matter how tempting it may be to accept a contract to carry a full load to a distant destination, the journey rapidly loses its profitability if there is no return load and the vehicle has to travel back empty.

Denby Transport is carefully managed, with each vehicle, and every journey that it makes, being monitored closely. Statistics have been calculated to establish what percentage of positioning mileage is permissible before viability is lost; vehicles are purchased according to an established strategy based on sound financial management; even the condition of used engine oil is monitored, and, of course, very accurate fuel records are kept. Fuel consumption is an important factor in profitability and is taken into account when buying new vehicles, and drivers are encouraged to aim for optimum fuel consumption. The company does all it can to enhance its drivers' skills. All drivers are regularly assessed by independent assessors, and re-training is provided

Top left: The founder of the Company, W.G. 'Bill' Denby. *Below:* The first fleet pictured together in the 1940s.

comfortable drivers are more alert. The drivers' appreciation of this little luxury can be deduced from their alacrity in reporting any fault with the air conditioning.

The current fleet includes box vans, curtainsiders, flats, low-loaders and trailers, so it can cope with most loads and meet most warehouses' loading requirements. Perhaps the most unusual load ever carried was a cargo

where needed. The company also employs the truck manufacturer's own instructors to give instruction on how to drive each particular model; this takes place a month after a new truck has been delivered, in order to give the driver time to accustom himself to the vehicle and its controls and so be ready and receptive to detailed instruction.

One investment to which the company committed itself six years ago is the provision of air conditioning throughout the fleet. This policy was instigated by Dick Denby, who had the idea while stuck on a French motorway for a considerable length of time during a heatwave; he happened to be in a car which had air conditioning, and stayed cool and comfortable whilst all the drivers around him were suffering from the heat. The company is convinced that the expense of fitting air conditioning is worthwhile; it is part of the company policy of looking after its drivers, and there is no doubt that cool,

consisting of two dinosaurs who travelled from Lincoln to Seville, Spain, on the open backs of low-loaders. The company is also fully certificated to carry hazardous chemicals, having become the first non-tanker UK haulier to pass the European chemical industry's safety and quality assessment; it also holds the ISO 9002.

Denby Transport remains a family business. In addition to Dick and Peter Denby, Elisabeth Denby, Dick's wife, is a Director in charge of warehousing and environmental issues and Caroline, Peter's sister, is Quality Manager. Denby Transport will continue to meet future challenges in its own careful and efficient manner, providing an added value service to its many customers at home and abroad.

Top left: One of the earliest low-loaders carrying a loading shovel made by Ruston Bucyrus in Lincoln.
Below: Three generations of the family pictured from left to right; Peter Denby, his sister Caroline Dickinson, Elisabeth Denby, Dick Denby and in front are Charlie Denby, Peter's son with Caroline's children Charlotte and Kit.

The company built up by skilled craftsmen

In 1944 a Public Works Order was issued to W and J Simons, a Nottingham firm of builders set up by Jimmy Abbott and his father William in 1873 and subsequently bought by Jimmy's son-in-law J L Booth, making it responsible for the maintenance of Lincoln's military airfields. J L Booth accordingly sent his promising 19-year old trainee surveyor Peter Hodgkinson to Lincoln, where, assisted by Harry Dunn, he set up an operations centre in a wooden hut in Friar's Lane. Towards the end of the war, when the firm was struggling to find enough work to stay in business, it was Harry Dunn's inspiration which saved the firm: thinking about the forthcoming Allied invasion of the Continent, he started imagining how many packing cases would be needed to transport equipment. So J L Booth, together with a local ironmonger called Sidney Coggins, put in a tender and submitted a sample case, and soon Simons was churning out

packing cases by the thousand; the company survived the war, and Harry Dunn was nicknamed the Box King.

The post-war years provided plenty of re-building work, and local authorities wanted new schools, hospitals and other institutions; Peter Hodgkinson proved adept at winning contracts, and the challenge then was to strike up good relationships with suppliers in order to obtain building materials which were scarce. This the firm successfully did, and contracts undertaken at that time included a girls' residence for the Lincoln Training College, the first building in Lincoln to have under-floor heating. The company's workforce grew; one of their new recruits was Nellie, a shabby three-wheeled truck which for six years was the only transport for the kit of plumbing department's five or six plumbing teams. Its joinery facility also expanded with the purchase in 1954 of E E Scarborough, a small joinery and jobbing works in Woodstock Street. Another firm, Mayfields, builders and

Top left: Albert Roberts beside the plumbing department's first van, Nellie the three wheeler. Right: Peter Hodgkinson pictured in the early 1980s.
Far Right: Pioneering the use of pumped concrete for the floor of the bedroom wing of the White Hart Hotel, Lincoln in the 1970s, overshadowed by the magnificent Lincoln Cathedral.

The recession of the 70s and early 80s hit the building industry hard, but Simons managed to survive and even undertook the ambitious project of purchasing and renovating Lincoln's Corn Exchange. Harry Dunn had by this time retired from Simons of Lincoln, maintaining his shareholding with the Northampton company, and Peter Hodgkinson's four sons were becoming involved in the business, with Martin and Philip working within the company, and Andrew forming the Simons Design Consultants as part of the Simons Group, where Paul joined him after qualifying as an architect. On 3rd December 1986, having successfully managed the company for 42 years, Peter Hodgkinson suffered a massive heart attack and died, and Paul took over as Chairman. Under his guidance growth has continued. Today the business is run by Paul and Philip Hodgkinson and is recognised nationally as one of the leading suppliers of construction, property development and consultancy services. Its client list reads like the FTSE 100, but with many of the customers still relating back to those early days in Lincoln. Indeed their supply chain, also often Lincoln based, has grown with them and helps to maintain the £150m turnover. Simons aim simply to be the "first choice" for customers, suppliers and employees, and to continue their tradition of excellent service and projects.

Top left: The Corn Exchange in Lincoln, completely refurbished in 1984, following eight years of work.
Below: The St. Marks development in Lincoln, completed in 1999. This project is used by the DOE as indicative of the way forward in planning.

undertakers of Sutton-on-Sea, was also acquired, and for the next few years the company prospered at the three sites under J L Booth's guidance; his insistence on the value of repeat business was without doubt a factor in that prosperity, and this is still a major part of Simons business philosophy today.

By the end of the 1950s the Lincoln outfit, under Peter Hodgkinson and Harry Dunn, was being run as a separate enterprise, carrying out maintenance work as well as new building contracts, and in 1964 it was agreed that the businesses should separate.

Simons of Lincoln, as it became, began to pursue a policy of expansion and soon earned a reputation for its aggressive approach and ferocious efficiency. The appointment of Gordon McIntyre as company accountant gave the firm the sound financial management needed to cope with expansion, and major contracts, such as construction of a new factory for Smiths' Crisps, the extraordinary extension to the Theatre Royal in York and a new office block for Terry's of York, soon followed. The company had by this time moved into its new Monks Road offices. During the early 70s, encouraged by its success in obtaining contracts in Yorkshire, the firm set up a subsidiary in Leeds, followed by branches in King's Lynn, Sleaford, Scunthorpe, Chester and Grimsby, and even one in Gibraltar which operated for 10 years before being sold back to local management.

The children of St Faith's Infants School celebrate the Coronation of Elizabeth II

Acknowledgments

Angela Child and the staff of the Local Studies department of
Lincoln County Library

The work of TC Hopkins and
the work of L Elvin

Thanks are also due to:
Kevin McIlroy who penned the editorial text and
Margaret Wakefield for her copywriting skills